Play Readings

D1598924

Play Readings: A Complete Guide for Theatre Practitioners demystifies the standards and protocols of play readings, demonstrating how to create useful and evocative readings for those new to or experienced with the genre. The book analyzes all of the essential elements involved in readings, including prerehearsal preparations, playwright/director/producer communications, editing/adapting stage directions, and using limited rehearsal time effectively. Simple suggestions for "staging," the use of music stands, casting considerations, and arguments surrounding talkbacks are examined in detail. A model for play readings is proposed, and diagrams and photographs illuminate the study for a comprehensive coverage of this increasingly prevalent form.

- Thought-provoking quotes from interviews with top theatre professionals which demonstrate the diversity and vibrancy of this nearly inevitable step in new play development.
- Detailed investigation of how to present various types of readings, including readings of new plays, nondevelopmental readings, and readings of new musicals and operas.
- Useful information for playwrights, directors, actors, producers, and audiences about all aspects of play readings from submission policies to follow-up discussions.

Rob Urbinati is a freelance director and playwright based in New York City, and Director of New Play Development at Queens Theatre. In New York, he has directed for Pearl Theater, The Public Theater, Classic Stage Company, York Theatre, The Culture Project, Abingdon Theatre, Ensemble Studio Theatre, Cherry Lane Theatre, and New York University. He has also directed at theatres and universities across the country. Rob's plays include "Hazelwood Jr. High," "West Moon Street," and "Death By Design," published by Samuel French. "Rebel Voices," "Cole Porter's Nymph Errant," and "The Queen Bees" will also be published by Samuel French. Other plays include "UMW," "Karaoke Night at the Suicide Shack," and "Mama's Boy." His plays have received over 100 productions world-wide. Rob is an alumnus of the Drama League Directors Project and the Lincoln Center Theater Directors Lab.

Play Readings

A Complete Guide for Theatre Practitioners

Rob Urbinati

Focal Press
Taylor & Francis Group

NEW YORK AND LONDON

First published 2016
by Focal Press
70 Blanchard Road, Suite 402, Burlington, MA 01803

and by Focal Press
2 Park Square, Milton Park, Abingdon, Oxon OX14 4RN

Focal Press is an imprint of the Taylor & Francis Group, an informa business

Notices

Knowledge and best practice in this field are constantly changing. As new research and experience broaden our understanding, changes in research methods, professional practices, or medical treatment may become necessary.

Practitioners and researchers must always rely on their own experience and knowledge in evaluating and using any information, methods, compounds, or experiments described herein. In using such information or methods they should be mindful of their own safety and the safety of others, including parties for whom they have a professional responsibility.

Product or corporate names may be trademarks or registered trademarks, and are used only for identification and explanation without intent to infringe.

Library of Congress Cataloging-in-Publication Data
Urbinati, Rob.
  Play readings : a complete guide for theatre practitioners / Rob Urbinati.
    pages cm
  Includes index.
  1. Theater rehearsals. 2. Theater—Production and direction. 3. Acting. I. Title.
  PN2071.R45U93 2015
  792.02′8—dc23
  2015014185

ISBN: 978-1-138-84130-7 (pbk)
ISBN: 978-1-138-84128-4 (hbk)
ISBN: 978-1-315-73232-9 (ebk)

Typeset in Sabon
by Apex CoVantage, LLC

Printed and bound in the United States of America by
Edwards Brothers Malloy on sustainable sourced paper

CONTENTS

ACKNOWLEDGEMENTS AND CREDITS

Interviewees

Anthony Arnove, Editor; Author; Producer
Nan Barnett, Executive Director, National New Play Network
Jesse Berger, Artistic Director, Red Bull Theater
James Bundy, Dean/Artistic Director, Yale School of Drama/Yale Repertory Theatre
Jason Cannon, Associate Artist, Florida Studio Theatre
Anne Cattaneo, Dramaturg, Lincoln Center Theater
Barry Childs, Administrative Director, The Other Side of Silence (TOSOS); Director
Lynn Cohen, Actor
Nick Connaughton, Creative Entertainment Manager, Arcola Theatre, London
Nick Corley, Director; Actor
Julie Crawford, Executive Director, American Association of Community Theatre
Ted deChatalet, Fight Choreographer; Director; Actor; Professor, Western Oregon University
Elaine Devlin, Agent
Gino DiIoria, Playwright
David Esbjornsen, Director
Dan Fields, Creative Director, Walt Disney Imagineering Creative Entertainment
Hayley Finn, Associate Artistic Director, Playwright's Center, Minneapolis; Director
Elizabeth Frankel, Director of New Work, The Alley Theatre; former Literary Manager, The Public Theater
Phil Funkenbusch, Director, Shows Division, Abraham Lincoln Presidential Library and Museum
Adam Greenfield, Associate Artistic Director, Playwrights Horizons
Janet Gupton, Director; Professor, Linfield College
Rajiv Joseph, Playwright
Nancy Lee-Painter, The Kennedy Center American College Theater Festival National Playwriting Program Vice-Chair, Region 7; Associate Professor of Theatre, Lewis-Clark State College
Amy Rose Marsh, Literary Manager, Samuel French, Inc.
Julie Mollenkamp, The Kennedy Center American College Theatre Festival National Playwriting Program Chair, Region 5
Ian Morgan, Associate Artistic Director, New Group
James Morgan, Producing Artistic Director, York Theatre Company
Kevin Newbury, Director
Don Nguyen, Playwright

Susan Louise O'Connor, Actor
A. Rey Pamatmat, Playwright
Laura Penn, Executive Director, Society of Stage Directors and Choreographers
Horacio Pérez, Producer; Director
Will Pomerantz, Director
Cara Reichel, Producing Artistic Director, Prospect Theater Company
Lisa Rothe, Director of Offsite Programs and Partnerships, Lark Playwrights Center; Director
Tom Rowan, Resident Casting Director, Ensemble Studio Theatre; Playwright; Director
Jojo Ruf, Managing Director, Laboratory for Global Performance and Politics, Georgetown University; former Executive Director, National New Play Network
Ralph Sevush, Esq., Executive Director/Business and Legal Affairs, Dramatists Guild of America, Inc.
Kim T. Sharp, Literary Manager, Abingdon Theatre
Maria Somma, Director of Communications, Actors Equity Association
Caridad Svich, Playwright
Daniella Topol, Director
Lauren Yee, Playwright
Jose Zayas, Director

Special Thanks

Carolyn Balducci, Barry Childs, Teri Clark, Mary Julia Curtis, Mashuq Deen, Jeff Frasier, Lisa Garza, Joseph Kissane, Melissa Maxwell, Willy Mosquera, James Rogers, Jeffrey Rosenstock, Taryn Sacramone, Sharon Sobel, Gregory Thorson, Sy and Rochelle Wichel, Steven Wolf

Plays Used in the Text

"Death by Design" by Rob Urbinati. Contact: www.samuelfrench.com
"Under the Mango Tree" by Carmen Rivera. Contact: Ron Gwiazda, ron.gwiazda@abramsartny.com
"Salt in a Wound" by Melissa Maxwell. Contact: www.melissamaxwell.com
"Mama's Boy" by Rob Urbinati. Contact: Elaine Devlin, Edevlinlit@aol.com
"Samsara" by Lauren Yee. Contact: Antje Oegel, aogel@aoiagency.com
"The Flood." Music and Lyrics by Peter Mills, Book by Cara Reichel. Contact: Susan Gurman, susan@gurmanagency.com

Photograph Credits

5.2   Adrianna Dufay, Steve Wolf, James Rogers, Kelly Feustel, Shawn Riley, Jeff Frazier
5.3   Jack King
5.4   Anita King
5.5   José Hernández
5.7   (left to right) Beatrice Gallagher, Gladys Bregenzer
5.10 (left to right) Beatrice Gallagher, John Gallagher, Gladys Bregenzer
5.11–5.17 Angelica Avilés, Imran Sheikh

8.13   (and all "Under the Mango Tree" photographs): Maribel Mota, Ronald Pina, Angelica Avilés, Brittney Haynes, Imran Sheikh, Sharon Walton, Gustavo Romero

9.1   (and all "Death by Design" photographs); Edna H. Greene, Shawn Riley, Melissa Maxwell, John Gallagher, Adrianna Dufay, James Rogers, Jeff Frazier, Beatrice Gallagher

9.14   (and all "Salt in a Wound" photographs): Norma Blanco, Jeff Frazier

9.16   (and all "Mama's Boy" photographs): Steve Wolf, Kelly Feustel

9.26   (and all "Samsara" photographs): José Hernández, Gustavo Romero, Maribel Mota, Imran Sheikh, Melissa Maxwell

Cover, Diagrams and Photography by Adrianna Dufay and Mac Premo with assistance from Divya Gadangi

Technical Editor: Daniela Varon

PREFACE

Play Readings: A Complete Guide for Theatre Practitioners is the first book on the subject; the scope is narrow, but the attempt is to be comprehensive within the scope. Some who read this book may never have seen or been involved with a Play Reading.

Having experienced Readings at every type of institution that presents them—professional theatres, community theatres, developmental labs, festivals, schools, conferences, literary societies, museums, and libraries—I believe that the observations contained here can be helpful to emerging, mid-career, and professional theatre artists.

The book is not advocacy. I accept the current model of new play development, which includes Play Readings, as a given and prefer Readings that are presented in ways that benefit playwrights and serve the needs of the various producing organizations. This book proposes guidelines for how this can be done, but there is no right way. Each play poses unique demands.

I interviewed early career and established playwrights, directors, actors, producers, artistic directors, dramaturgs, literary managers, and union representatives. They have fascinating—and contrasting—ideas. Their opinions often contradict one other and contradict my own preferences. I am grateful for their passion and the intellectual rigor of their insights. I learned a great deal from our discussions.

I deliberately solicited opposing voices. These insights, included throughout the book, remind theatre artists that divergent approaches to new play development must be explored.

I have lived in New York most of my adult life. The city has shaped my knowledge and opinions of theatre, and many of the artists interviewed are based in New York City. However, it is not my intention to position the city as the epicenter of new plays; the book argues against that.

Play Readings are only a component of contemporary new play development, a large, encompassing subject. More studies are needed to examine the current models—how they began, how they evolved, how they are changing, and how they must be continuously adapted and improved.

The book does not explore the business, economics, or industry of play production and just touches upon the challenges that confront playwrights. These are complex issues, worthy of study, and beyond the scope of this book.

While the book privileges playwrights—*all* playwrights, alternative and mainstream—I have deep respect for participants at every stage of play development, including the audience. They take pride in the roles they play and recognize their responsibility to writers.

I admit to biases. But rules are made to be broken. All theatre artists are in this together, working toward the same goal.

INTRODUCTION

Play Readings and New Play Development

On any given week, across the country and around the world, hundreds—perhaps thousands—of Play Readings are presented to audiences. Forty years ago, there was likely a handful. New work offered to the public in the form of Readings has grown into an international phenomenon and an almost inevitable step on the path to full production.

Many professional theatres include Reading series as part of their new play programs. Play Readings are among the various approaches used by developmental labs. Many of the more than fifty theatres that are Core or Associate Members of the National New Play Network present Readings at their gatherings. The National Alliance for Musical Theatre and the ASCAP Musical Theatre Workshops prominently feature Readings of new musicals. American Lyric Theater and American Opera Company present Readings and Workshops of operas in development. The Kennedy Center American College Theater Festival, a national program that involves nearly 20,000 students, presents Readings of plays of all lengths at its regional and national festivals. Many of the 1,200 Member Theatres of the American Association of Community Theatre, an organization that has increased its advocacy of new plays, program Play Readings. Even the Educational Theatre Association's annual Thespian Festival, an organization of high school teachers and students, presents Readings of new works.

The prominence of Readings as a step in new play development has implications for playwrights and every theatre artist involved. Producers and artistic directors at many theatres determine programming based on the perceived success of a Play Reading. Who will direct and perform in the full production are decisions often influenced by Readings. Winners of playwriting competitions receive exposure through Readings at festivals. Audiences develop their critical skills by attending work in development. Play Readings impact the shape and direction of contemporary theatre.

Readings are absolutely essential to the development of my plays. I compare writing a play to writing a piece of music for several instruments—say a chamber orchestra. I can write till I'm blue in the face, but eventually I have to hear some musicians play the notes. And that's what readings are all about. Immediately I hear

*the places where the music stops making sense, where it goes off
key, where something predictable happens.*

*I have never, ever found a reading to be unhelpful. I always
strive to find ways to make one happen—whether through the
Lark Play Development Center, which is committed to this
process—or simply on my own, by bringing friends together in a
room and hearing them read my latest draft aloud.*

Rajiv Joseph, Playwright

History of New Play Development

Throughout theatre history, playwrights have had associations with theatres that
presented their work; William Shakespeare, Anton Chekhov, Eugene O'Neill,
Bertolt Brecht, Clifford Odets, and many others wrote for specific companies
and, in some cases, specific actors. Certain directors have had long-term collaboration with particular playwrights, helping shape their plays, as with Elia Kazan
and Tennessee Williams. The dynamics of these relationships are distinct and
occasionally obscure. Clearly, many writers wrote alone, without guidance or
support from theatres or directors. Any Reading of the play was private, for the
playwright, director, producer, and actors.

Although small theatres existed earlier in the twentieth century, the growth
of alternative venues for new plays flourished in the 1950s. The upsurge in this
Off-Broadway and, more significantly, Off-Off-Broadway scene transformed the
ways in which new plays were presented. Off-Off-Broadway thrived on alternative work; with rebellious abandon, first drafts were thrown onstage, and actors
were said to be pulled off the street. Influential companies such as Caffé Cino,
LaMama Experimental Theatre Club, Theatre Genesis, and Judson Poets' Theatre were venues for new, experimental plays. Open Theater and Living Theatre created politically charged pieces specifically for their companies, reflecting
the social upheavals of the period. The Off-Off-Broadway movement offered
a vibrant alternative to Broadway. Unlike the contemporary model, it did not
develop plays—it produced them.

The shape and direction of current new play development was formulated in
the late 1960s and 1970s with the influx of grants and funding, along with regulations by Actors Equity Association. The Off-Off-Broadway scene declined, as
nonprofit theatres in New York City advanced. Unlike the commercial Broadway
business model that was becoming increasingly expensive with fewer and fewer
plays produced each year, nonprofit theatres presented limited runs of plays, and
earned income rolled back into the institution. The Negro Ensemble Company,
Ensemble Studio Theatre, The Circle Repertory Company, and Playwrights Horizons, among others, formed a vital community of playwright-driven theatres
consisting of small collectives of artists pledged to creating new work. Many
playwrights flourished in these nurturing environments. Early development labs
such as The Eugene O'Neill Theatre Center also launched in this period, offering
writers a place to work without the pressure of production.

As a result of the competition for funding and increased production costs, theatres and labs recognized a need to improve quality. A commitment to developing
plays began, with Readings as part of the process. In-house Readings were held
for invited audiences of staff and colleagues. Playwrights had always received
input from directors and producers, but as the nonprofit theatre scene grew,

teams of dramaturgs and literary managers within these companies joined the conversation.

In the 1980s, the explosion of nonprofit theatres in New York and elsewhere intensified the demand for new plays. What had been a comparatively small group of companies focusing on new work burst into a national movement. Soon, play development programs were established at nonprofit theatres across the country, and playwrights received substantially more advice on their work. The 1990s saw an increase in nonproducing development labs. The inspiration to develop new work spread to theatre festivals, community theatres, conferences, and other organizations.

A major shift had occurred. New plays were now often viewed as drafts that required input or assistance from various sources to realize their potential.

As interest flourished, more voices joined the conversation. Many theatre artists believed that a general audience's response to a play might be instructive in the early stages of development. Play Readings, which had previously been In-house, were now open to the public. Reading series of new plays became a programming component at many nonprofit theatres. Playwrights, producers, directors, dramaturgs, and a literary staff observed and assessed the response. No policies or guidelines existed for how these public Readings were presented. For most of the artists involved, participating in a Play Reading in the 1980s was on-the-job training.

In addition to intuiting audience response, some theatres began to actively solicit their opinions through talkbacks following the Reading. Playwrights were now encouraged—and at times required—to field comments and suggestions from a general audience of theatregoers. The volume of counsel a playwright receives through contemporary models of development is staggering.

Dissenting Voices

The soundness of the current new play landscape is not unchallenged.

Some theatre artists argue that small companies of like-minded peers have been replaced by institutions with a corporate approach. The personal connection that benefited playwrights as part of communities of artists is difficult to achieve when the writer is merely one player on the team.

In the late seventies, everything was connected and convivial. Theatre artists were forging new paths, creating new communities of writers at theatres. Ensemble Studio Theatre, Circle Rep, Playwrights Horizons, the NEC—they consisted of groups of equal peers who saw the world the same way. The main thing was that they knew each other. The playwrights had agency. Their peers listened to them. This type of organic professionalism works best for creating new plays. Then the new play process became a shopping mall. Regional theatres wanted to pick up the new, hot plays from NY new play theaters, from the O'Neill. AEA's newly instituted showcase code, which asked playwrights whose productions transferred to reimburse the actors not taken along had a dampening effect. Theatre became an adjunct of our celebrity culture. Now, every city has a theatre with a huge operating budget. Boards of course require that theatres bring in millions a year to keep their buildings and staffs solvent. And the personal connection isn't there. This is what's changed. Theatre is no longer created by friends. I encourage emerging writers and directors to work with their friends—to start making things. Build relationships. Work in ways that you're comfortable with. It's all about trust and intimacy.

Anne Cattaneo, Dramaturg, Lincoln Center Theater

Most producers, playwrights, and directors agree that traditional, well-made plays benefit most from Play Readings. Theatrical or experimental work is not well served by the model. Even naturalistic plays involving physical action are difficult to present as Play Readings, which may impact their production prospects.

Plays Served by Readings

Readings gratify the ear, not the eye. They privilege a certain kind of play, one that's linguistically rich, not necessarily theatrically rich. And magnificent performers can paint over underlying weaknesses, obscuring judgment.

James Bundy, Dean/Artistic Director,
Yale School of Drama/Yale Repertory Theatre

When I hear a play reading that zips along with huge, unbridled audience response, I get nervous. I consider it a potential warning sign if the actors and the audience can access the play too easily. If what is on the page is instantly understood then it might be lacking the complexity or depth to ultimately hold an audience in the theatre.

David Esbjornsen, Director

Not every play is intended to have a reading. Plays which incorporate media or dance, that require visual language or movement are still plays, but not really digestible in terms of spoken language. Some people write plays for readings, but these plays don't always perform as well in production. Should writers make their plays "reading-proof"? That's not what a play is about. Play readings can be slightly dangerous territory.

Caridad Svich, Playwright

The plays that I love the most—that I respect the most, would fail at public readings.

Anne Cattaneo, Dramaturg, Lincoln Center Theater

Talkbacks are particularly controversial, with audiences often seen as adversaries.

> *We never do talkbacks after readings—only after performances. They are a crapshoot, and can be a waste of time. Most writers dread talkbacks. They prefer to discuss the reading with friends, colleagues and the artistic staff.*
> Elizabeth Frankel, Literary Manager,
> The Public Theater

Playwrights have always solicited advice from their collaborators, peers, and colleagues. But in the current environment, a playwright must weigh suggestions from producers, directors, dramaturgs, literary staff, playwriting program chairs, readers, respondents, and audiences. Most plays have many Readings, which compound the volume of input. "Development Hell" is a well-worn phrase used for plays that have had multiple Readings or Workshops over a period of years and have not advanced to full production.

> *Development should not become perpetual. The play will be watered down. Serving too many masters is an inherent danger in development. It's best when playwrights are empowered. They should be given the tools so that they can make their own decisions. They shouldn't be expected to follow precepts. But even when done incorrectly, the process can be helpful. From this, you learn how to do it correctly.*
> Ralph Sevush, Esq., Executive Director/Business and
> Legal Affairs, Dramatists Guild of America, Inc.

How do contemporary writers handle the voluminous comments they now receive from multiple sources? How can they maintain their vision and integrity through the lengthy process of development? How do they separate insightful ideas from useless suggestions? How do they handle the demands placed upon them? To whom should they listen?

> *Beware of trying to answer everyone's questions, or take everyone's suggestions. Once when I did this, my play became sturdier, clearer—maybe even more robust—but it lost a layer of magic. Playwrights have to use development to learn about themselves as a writer—how to be present in a room with collaborators. Now, I give myself permission not to solve every problem with every reading. I choose specific things to look at.*
> Don Nguyen, Playwright

In contemporary theatre in the English-speaking world, very few new plays receive full productions without having first been presented to the public in a Play Reading. To maneuver effectively in this terrain, the purpose of any Reading or developmental step must be clear to everyone involved.

Goals

If you're going to do a reading, it's important to have very specific questions. Be clear about why you're doing it; and do it in order to find something specific. For example, with some plays, your goal might be to find how the humor works. Or how a "choreographed" sequence, or a series of rapid sequences work. That's always a good reason to do a reading: to explore a particular issue.

Adam Greenfield, Associate Artistic Director,
Playwrights Horizons

It's important for the collaborators to have a frank discussion of the collective goal before any stage of development. Why are we doing this? Is it an exploratory process, or is it about a polished product?

Cara Reichel, Producing Artistic Director,
Prospect Theater Company

Where readings get confusing is when the agendas get mixed up. Is it an early incubation, where the writer wants to try out new pages, sort out what they've written and where they want to go next? Or is about how to land a production? You think it's an early reading, and then everyone invites producers. Writers can regret inviting people too early. Ultimately, a play reading is always an audition, unless a production is already scheduled. Then it's a pre-production reading, which is entirely different. So it's good to be super clear about what the purpose is.

Daniella Topol, Director

To function in a Reading-centric climate, playwrights must learn to use Readings for their own purposes. Directors and actors, with limited rehearsal time, must illuminate the playwright's text simply and effectively to tell the story, communicate the style, reveal the characters, and convey dramatic intention with purpose and clarity. Producers must use Readings in ways that benefit the writer—and hopefully provide other resources to help develop new work.

Some producers rely extensively on public Readings and audience response to choose which plays they will produce. But a well-presented Reading can disguise a play's shortcomings, while an ineffective Reading may be the result of factors other than the play. The quality of the presentation will impact audience response as much as the quality of the play itself.

Readings and Programming

At Yale Rep, there is no machinery through which we march all new plays. Playwrights have input in all of the decisions about their work. We are led by, and embrace playwrights' and directors' perspectives.

We don't use readings to decide whether or not to produce a play. If a playwright wants a reading—if that's what they really want, we'll do one. But maybe it's an in-house reading of the first act, with just actors and director. Readings shouldn't be used as a test. They should be for the artist, not to determine producorial interest.

James Bundy, Dean/Artistic Director,
Yale School of Drama/Yale Repertory Theatre

Readings are part of a play's development, but they are rarely used for programming. If we all read a play and fall in love with it, a reading isn't necessary. More often than not, readings are not "make or break" moments at the Public. They are a step on the path to development.

Elizabeth Frankel, Literary Manager,
The Public Theater

At New Group, we don't make decisions about what to produce from readings. They are for our own artistic purposes, and the playwrights'. Readings should never be determinative.

Ian Morgan, Associate Artistic Director, New Group

While programming decisions at the theatres and organizations I've been involved with are influenced by the quality of the readings, the quality of the play is more important. This is why we have such strict aesthetic expectations for readings and have so many different levels of readings. If you don't have a baseline, then how can you compare? So we hold ourselves accountable, ensure that all readings are of high quality, and then we can focus more on the quality of the play itself and find the scripts that we want to actively pursue, develop, and ultimately produce. That's the whole reason for development and readings: to find great plays to fully produce for our audience.

Jason Cannon, Associate Artist, Florida Studio Theatre

Prospect Theater Company develops new musicals that we believe in—musicals that we are interested in producing, or that we've decided to produce. We've already made a commitment. We do not undertake readings to audition material. We do readings to support the artists, because we believe in their voice, and have confidence in the piece and want to provide an opportunity for it to grow.

Cara Reichel, Producing Artistic Director,
Prospect Theater Company

You don't need to hear a play to determine whether it has value but it may be the way to decide if it has a theatrical future. For better or for worse, it is often the way producers make decisions. It is completely valid to hear the play out loud but I personally don't always

> *trust that an audience response is any indication of success at the box office. The best producers tend to go with their instincts.*
>
> David Esbjornsen, Director
>
> *Readings should not be auditions for productions. So much can go wrong. An actor might be miscast. There's usually not enough rehearsal time to follow an idea through to its completion. And a play should not be asked to stand up to all the potential failings of a reading. A writer can say, "I need to hear it." That's fine. But it's not for the producer to say.*
>
> Adam Greenfield, Associate Artistic Director,
> Playwrights Horizons

Scope and Purpose

Dissenting voices notwithstanding, the model of development in which Readings play a prominent role continues to flourish. This book makes no argument for or against Play Readings as part of any new play development process. Their advantages and challenges are assessed so playwrights can make informed decisions that serve their individual purposes.

The goal of this book is to provide playwrights, directors, actors, composers, lyricists, librettists, producers, dramaturgs, literary managers, festival coordinators, curators of museums and literary societies, and other theatre practitioners of all levels of experience with helpful suggestions about how best to convey the creators' intentions in Readings of new plays, musicals, and operas. The guidelines should be adapted to suit the specific needs of these works.

This book makes a case for Play Readings as a distinct theatrical form separate from the full productions of those plays, recognizing that most Readings are a step toward production, not a substitute.

> *I have been privileged to observe some play readings that I actually preferred to the staged production that followed. Beyond the magic of this moment of discovering a play, I find that some actors' initial instincts in a reading the script are more truthful than the direction they take their performance (or are directed to take). They tend to be more respectful of the text. The structure also compels actors to listen to the rest of the cast with a particular attentiveness.*
>
> Anthony Arnove, Editor; Author; Producer

Definition of Terms

Readings of new plays, musicals, and operas are programmed by institutions across the country and around the world for their audiences, members, and participants. No standardized policies exist for how Play Readings are presented, even within the organizations themselves, which often adapt their methods to respond to the needs of a given work and to serve their own needs.

Theatres

The term is used in this book to describe institutions that primarily produce new plays, including many nonprofit professional theatres and some community theatres.

Developmental Labs

Labs are devoted exclusively to the development of new plays, musicals, and operas, providing resources to writers and composers. Unlike theatres, production is not the goal. In lab settings, playwrights often decide how to use their time. Residencies and commissions are common. The Playwrights' Center in Minneapolis and American Lyric Theatre are examples of developmental labs.

Other Organizations

Recent years have seen the growth of organizations dedicated wholly or in part to the development of new plays. They are networks, alliances, programs, festivals, and associations that provide resources and exposure for professional, nonprofessional, and academic theatre artists. While these organizations develop new work and may provide routes to production, the organizations themselves do not produce. In this book, "organization" is a catch-all term for such diverse institutions as the National New Play Network and The Kennedy Center American College Theater Festival.

Literary Staff

Most institutions that produce, present, or develop new work have individuals on staff who read new plays and confer with playwrights in the early stages of development. Artistic directors may participate at this level, but many are not involved until later in the process. The literary staff can consist of dramaturgs, directors of new play development, associate artistic directors, literary managers, literary committees, and readers.

Types of Readings

Various terminologies exist for the many types of Readings currently offered. Some of the language is vague or misleading. Below is an attempt to establish a nomenclature that will be used throughout this book.

Cold Reading

Cold Reading is a term used most frequently for auditions in which an actor is presented with a scene or monologue for the first time and reads it without preparation. Occasionally, In-house Readings of new plays, discussed below, can be Cold Readings, but most playwrights prefer that the actors familiarize themselves with the script in advance to avoid simple mistakes. In a Cold Reading, actors make impromptu interpretive choices. A Cold Reading should not be presented to the public.

In-house Reading (or Table Reading)

Actors are gathered by a theatre, lab, or other organization for an informal Reading of a new play or a new draft. Friends and colleagues may attend, as well as the producer, artistic director, and literary staff. In-house Readings are generally performed without rehearsal. They are not open to the public.

Reading a play to oneself is essentially a literary experience, even for those with vivid imaginations. Language, plot, character, tone, rhythm, and style can be illuminated when the play is spoken, which may lead to useful rewrites. Hearing the play, most writers experience the dialogue, rhythm, and dramatic action in ways that might not have been apparent when writing. The playwright may also consider the responses of the artists involved and begin to assemble a team of collaborators.

An early draft of a new play is often better served by a private, In-house Reading than a public Reading. The goals of In-house Readings differ considerably and reflect the needs of the producing organization, the playwright, and the play. An In-house Reading relieves the pressure of a public performance.

Staged Reading

The term is often used for Play Readings, which is misleading as it implies that these Readings will be staged; in most cases, they are not. Previously, most Readings of new plays were referred to as Staged Readings, but the phrase is on the wane. Theatre artists are aware that staging a full production takes weeks or months. If a producer requests staging, more rehearsal time should be offered. If the Reading incorporates blocking and the cast does not use music stands, the term "Staged Reading" is appropriate.

Script-in-hand Reading

Given that scripts are placed on music stands at many Play Readings, this term is often a misnomer. Script-in-hand Reading is a rather cumbersome phrase, what with all those hyphens.

Concert Reading, Reading of a New Musical, and Reading of a New Opera

Concert Reading is an unclear term. In many parts of the country, it is used interchangeably with Play Reading or Staged Reading, likely because of the use of music stands. However, Readings of plays should be distinguished from Readings of musicals or operas, and the term Concert Reading suggests music. Concert Reading also implies that the performance will feature an orchestra, which may not be the case. The best use of the term Concert Reading is for a Reading of a new musical or opera with an orchestra. "Reading of a New Musical" or "Reading of a New Opera" are the terms used herein, with or without an orchestra.

Readings of musicals and operas require more rehearsal time for the singers and musicians to familiarize themselves with the score. Additional artistic staff is involved, including the composer; lyricist; librettist; musical director or conductor; and, at times, a vocal arranger, an orchestrator, a choreographer, a chorus, and an orchestra.

Nondevelopmental Reading

The term is used in this book to include Readings of plays or musicals performed for benefits, galas, fundraisers, or special events, as well as Readings of published, classic, or neglected plays often presented as part of a theatre's general programming. Readings of selections from novels or nonfiction works are also included in this category. While many Play Readings are free of charge, tickets may be sold for Nondevelopmental Readings. The presentations are often, but not always, an end unto themselves, with no further production intended.

Industry Reading

Formerly known as a backers' audition, often held in someone's home, Industry Readings, which now take place in theatres or rehearsal halls, can be Play Readings, Staged Readings, or Workshops and are by invitation only for potential producers, artistic directors, donors, investors, and other theatre insiders.

Workshop

An imprecise term used for a Staged Reading, or Reading of a New Musical or Opera that has a longer rehearsal period than a Play Reading. Sometimes known as a "Semi-Staged Reading," Workshops are often the developmental step that follows a Play Reading. Workshops can be either In-house or public. In addition to blocking, Workshops may include scenery and costumes and, in the case of musicals or operas, musicians and a chorus. A full array of minimally staged and designed presentations of musicals that are more than Readings but less than full productions has flourished of late.

Developmental Reading

Apart from Nondevelopmental Readings discussed above, every Reading of a new play, musical, or opera is a Developmental Reading in some way. The term is too vague for practical usage.

Play Reading (or Reading)

Play Readings are public performances of new work. They have a limited rehearsal period, usually from four hours to two days and occasionally as long as a week. A Reading provides a snapshot examination of the text at a specific moment in the play's development.

Actors are asked to review the script in advance but are not required to memorize lines.

Stage directions are read aloud, usually by an actor who is not portraying a character in the Reading.

Readings can be directed very simply, with actors sitting in chairs holding scripts, or more presentationally, with scripts on music stands and actors physically embodying the characters. Most Readings employ little if any staging or technical enhancement.

As public presentations, Play Readings allow the writer and others on the artistic team to assess the audience reaction during the performance and, in some cases, through talkbacks that follow.

Note: In this book, the term "producer" will be used for anyone who is in a position to offer a Reading to a playwright. "Stage manager" will refer to someone who assists with coordinating the Reading.

PART 1

BEFORE REHEARSALS

CHAPTER 1

GOING PUBLIC

Theatre is a public art. But when to "go public" with a new play is not an easy decision. Playwrights should believe their plays are ready for an audience before submitting them for a public Reading. In-house Readings and labs provide opportunities for writers to explore early drafts of new plays or ideas for new work. These are sound alternatives to public Play Readings. But at what point in its development might a play benefit from exposure to an audience?

> *Table reads, in-house Readings and public Readings all have value, with different benefits. Table Readings or in-house Readings are the best ways to translate the written word to the spoken word. They allow playwrights to hear how the words fall out of the actors' mouths. These types of private readings are for the playwright's benefit. Playwrights can hear what they want to accomplish. The benefit of public readings is that the audience response affects the rhythm of the piece, and impacts pacing. After laughter, there is a pause. You can only learn that in front of an audience.*
>
> Ralph Sevush, Esq., Executive Director/Business and Legal Affairs, Dramatists Guild of America, Inc.

Hearing their words spoken aloud, sitting among theatregoers, can illuminate the work in a variety of ways for writers. Many cherish this experience.

Playwrights

I find readings useful. I start with the kernel of a play, not knowing what it's about. Readings are an opportunity to explore. They hold me responsible. Readings impose a helpful deadline. I have to set goals for myself. The reality of actors makes me want to do my best work.

Lauren Yee, Playwright

Readings move something out of your head and make it external. Hearing your play out loud involves more than whether then dialogue sounds right, the actors are tripping over lines, or the jokes land—you can also access the subtext layer. Is the character too passive? Do they want something enough? No matter how well you know your play, you don't really know it till you've heard it read. I use the reading and development process to ask questions of myself.

Don Nguyen, Playwright

Public readings provide motivation. I learn if I'm onto something, if I should keep going. I had a reading of one of my plays once—a play I was unsure of, with a twist at the end. At the reading, the audience gasped—and I knew I had a play.

Gino DiIorio, Playwright

Working on public Readings, directors can acquire a deeper understanding of characters and relationships that may inform future casting choices. Questions or concerns formulated when the director examined the play may be emphasized or resolved. The Reading may spark ideas for a full production and expose challenges that staging the work might involve. Directors learn what they might expect from collaboration with the playwright and the producers.

Directors

Readings function as exploration or investigation. A good director usually knows whether the script is strong by reading it. But hearing actors perform the play can often affirm your instincts or in some instances alert you to potential problems. They also allow you to try out actors who you or the producer might be interested in. I find them useful in preparing for a production and less so as an exercise for producers. Although they usually only require a day of activity for the theatre they can often be weeks of "on the phone" or e-mail casting and will take up a lot of your time and psychic energy.

David Esbjornsen, Director

With a reading, you can do things simply that in a full production would cost a million dollars. Someone stands on a chair to represent flying. Done.

Nick Corley, Director; Actor

Listening to a Play Reading is akin to seeing that first pixilated sonogram of an unborn child. You can clearly see hands, fingers, a nose. Here is incontrovertible proof that there is indeed a baby!

Lisa Garza, Artistic Director, Houston Family
Arts Center; Director

It's important to hear the material out loud. Your brain processes information differently when you hear it through your ears than when you read it on the page.

Cara Reichel, Producing Artistic Director,
Prospect Theater Company

I can't imagine not doing workshops of projects that are in development. Everything we do at Imagineering goes through a significant development process before it goes into a venue. We spend a lot of time with the text for each project. Essentially, it's a discovery process. We examine the rhythm of the piece, from moment to moment and scene to scene. I need to hear the "music" of the piece—the highs and lows, the stops and starts, how a scene builds to a peak, releases, and then moves on. Until the dialogue comes out of actors' mouths, I feel I can't have an honest conversation with the writers.

Dan Fields, Creative Director, Walt Disney
Imagineering Creative Entertainment

You need a public reading to feel the energy in the room.

Daniella Topol, Director

Readings have many purposes beyond the old idea of "fixing the play." Readings can be presented for other purposes. They can simply be about the essence of storytelling. Or they can expand the palette of the audience, and get them accustomed to alternative material. Readings are also an access point for younger, less established directors.

Laura Penn, Executive Director, Society of Stage
Directors and Choreographers

An actor in a Reading is the first, or among the first, to lift the character off the page and give it voice. Without the luxury of time to explore their characters, actors make quick choices that can help writers learn if their intentions in the script are clear. Actors in Readings meet producers, playwrights, directors, and other actors and have their work seen by audiences.

Actors

Sometimes, I do as many as three readings a week. I think it's important. I care deeply. I have great respect for the writer. It is my contribution to the process.

Lynn Cohen, Actor

I enjoy the wild abandon of under-rehearsed public readings. They're gutsy. You don't have to worry about what decision you're going to make. There's less self-doubt and self-judging—you just jump into the pool! They're freeing, because you've already been given a "thumbs-up" by being asked to participate. Usually I don't request a script before accepting an offer. If I'm available, I'd rather be there than not there.

Susan Louise O'Connor, Actor

The producer, the artistic director, and the literary staff can experience the theatrical "event" of the play and assess its impact on the audience.

Producers

You can learn from the reading of a new musical. I try not to go in with a preconceived idea. Let the reading talk to you, and it's amazing what you may get from it.

James Morgan, Producing Artistic Director,
York Theatre Company

Public play readings are a must during development. It is vital to hear the audience's response. For playwrights, a reading is a great place to learn about an audience's response to a play—what works, what doesn't, where to make cuts, or when to eliminate or move a scene. They should watch rehearsals, listen, and be prepared to make changes both during the rehearsal and following the reading.

Nan Barnett, Executive Director,
National New Play Network

Plays need audiences. Writing is a lonely exercise, but unlike a novel, a play is ultimately collaborative, and readings jump-start that collaborative process. Readings don't tell playwrights what to write, but they do tell playwrights what is working, what is clear, what is confusing. Readings allow playwrights to test drive, test out, discover.

Jason Cannon, Associate Artist,
Florida Studio Theatre

TOSOS (The Other Side of Silence) began in 2002 with a series of staged readings at the LGBTQ Center in New York City, and readings in various forms continue to be an essential part of our mission and our season programming. Play readings allow our audiences to hear new works and new voices, and provide our member and associate playwrights with ongoing opportunities. We are also passionate about presenting plays from the past which we think are deserving of wider attention, especially plays that illuminate the history of LGBTQ lives, narratives and cultural heritage. Our readings are often events unto themselves, and we have an established audience that appreciates our one-of-a-kind offerings. Unsurprisingly, the majority of our productions started out as TOSOS readings. We remain committed to producing play readings so that we can provide playwrights with a forum where they can continue to share their stories with us.

Barry Childs, Administrative Director, TOSOS

Despite the opportunities they provide, some theatre artists find Readings risky and unnecessary.

Limitations

I don't always trust readings. They're not reliable. I think reading a play on the page, to myself, is closer to the experience of the play than a reading is. There's this idea that a reading adds dimensions. But really, a reading is an illusion of dimension. If you're good at reading plays, that experience is three-dimensional. I don't think I need to hear a play out loud to get it. I value the experience of reading plays. That's how I learned about theatre—by poring over plays.

Adam Greenfield, Associate Artistic Director,
Playwrights Horizons

I often feel that plays don't need readings—they need a smart person giving the writer feedback. Often, writers will say, "I want to get in the room with actors." But do you really need ten actors to make that rewrite? The reading model isn't always the only way forward.

Elizabeth Frankel, Literary Manager,
The Public Theater

The usefulness of readings is somewhat limited. Personally, I'd rather read a play, and imagine its possibilities. But when handled judiciously, a reading can be useful, particularly when the playwright knows what he or she is looking for.

Lisa Rothe, Director

Readings should not be an end to themselves. Readings should not be presented instead of productions, but to lead to productions.

Ralph Sevush, Esq., Executive Director/Business
and Legal Affairs, Dramatists Guild of America, Inc.

With most theatres, readings are a little dance. Producers aren't upfront about why they're doing the play. And I want to know. I can't stand pussyfooting around. Dealing with literary managers can be frustrating. I've had plays announced and then withdrawn without knowing why. What I want is candor. It's okay to say, "We have enhancement money for another play." But the silent treatment is crappy. And agents are trying to maintain relationships with the theatres, so they don't push for answers.

Gino DiIorio, Playwright

The danger is when theatre companies think that simply doing readings is the same as actual development. Readings are just one component of full-fledged development.

Jason Cannon, Associate Artist,
Florida Studio Theatre

The temptation to take readings too seriously should be avoided. You should never draw conclusions that are unwarranted. The reading isn't going to save anything. They can get you thinking, and get your creative juices flowing, but only if you discount a lot of things about them. And they can be dangerous for emerging writers. Yet so much of playwriting exists in a vacuum. And no playwright wants their work to exist in a vacuum. Readings are part of the process of collaboration that theatre is built on. The writer, director and actors get to know each other, and the theatre gets to know the playwright. Playwrights get to think about the play with a group of artists that they respect. But they have to consider the pitfalls. Playwrights need to learn how to use readings.

Ian Morgan, Associate Artistic Director, New Group

What would happen if we put a ten year moratorium on readings and commissions? It would force a change. Theatre people would have to rethink how plays are created. It would upend the process, which in need of upending. We all would give opportunities and money to writers but we would be forced to rethink how we do it, and perhaps we would do it in a way that gave the writers more agency.

Anne Cattaneo, Dramaturg, Lincoln Center Theater

Readings are a double-edged sword. While no one makes you have a reading, a culture of readings exists, and artistic directors and literary managers expect that a play will have had a reading, or multiple readings before it's produced.

Don Nguyen, Playwright

All theatre artists must develop the skills to separate the strengths and shortcomings of the play from the strengths and shortcomings of the Reading of that play. This is not easy. Even professional critics have trouble distinguishing the qualities of new plays from the productions of those plays, and a minimally rehearsed Play Reading can compound these challenges. Theatre artists must also learn what to listen for in a Reading, which may change with each play. These skills come from experience and from trusted teams of colleagues and collaborators.

Listening to a Play Reading

- Does the dialogue sound natural?
- Do passages with heightened language sound the way the writer intends?
- If an actor misinterprets the tone or intention of a line, can this be addressed simply with a stage direction preceding the line of dialogue, such as "playfully," or is a rewrite required?
- Was the audience restless when they should have been attentive?
- Did they laugh at the jokes?
- Were there other useful reactions or responses?
- Did the dramatic events unfold convincingly?
- Did the play "come to life" in the way the playwright, director, and producer envisioned?
- Were there challenges that were not apparent when the playwright, director, producer, and literary staff read the play?

CHAPTER 2

THE PRELIMINARIES

Submission Policies

It is an honor for playwrights to have their work selected for Play Readings. Theatres, labs, and other organizations receive hundreds of submissions, and the selection process is arduous. New plays pass through numerous steps of evaluation before the final decisions. One hopes that every work enters the process with an equal chance of being chosen.

Decisions are informed by more than the specific quality of the plays. Producers and artistic directors consider their theatres' missions and audiences' tastes, as well as the need to assemble a varied roster of plays. Cast size and costly production elements often influence the choices. Festival coordinators specify the length of the play, and competitions may have other restrictions. In all cases, requirements and procedures should be clearly stated in the submission policies.

Playwrights need to read submission policies and follow the instructions carefully. They should only submit work that fits into the parameters. Writers should also review mission statements and production histories. While it is the producers' duty to generate comprehensive submission policies, it is the playwrights' responsibility to fully research any institution before submitting their work. If the submission policies are unclear, playwrights can request additional information.

Where to Submit

When writers submit plays, they hope to receive an offer for a full production. That may happen, but rarely. More often, if the institution is interested in the work, developmental steps will precede production.

At certain theatres, plays will not be considered for full production without a Reading, even if the play has had multiple previous Readings. Writers may feel that the play has been read enough and nothing more can be gained. Playwrights who are not interested in a Reading should not submit the play where Readings are stipulated, just as actors who are only interested in principal roles should make their intentions clear when auditioning.

If the submission policy at any organization states that selected plays will receive a Reading, or if Readings are a component of that institution's programming, when a playwright submits the work, they have, in effect, agreed to a Reading. If they are contacted with an offer, they should accept.

When playwrights feel their work will not be well served by the limited rehearsal period of a standard Reading, they should explore other options. Most labs and, increasingly, many theatres do not require Readings. Some offer Workshops, commissions, and residencies. These venues are valuable alternatives for Reading-averse playwrights. Wisely, they leave the developmental approach to the writer.

The Offer

Information provided with an initial offer for a Play Reading varies. Some institutions include comprehensive details along with the offer. Many make the offer and details follow. If playwrights have not already agreed to a Reading by submitting, as discussed above, they may need more information before they accept. Eager to have their work seen, writers often agree to a Play Reading, later discovering stipulations or conditions.

> *Playwrights should know of any attachment or subsidiary rights.*
> *They should never give up subsidiary rights for anything less than*
> *a full professional production.*
> Ralph Sevush, Esq., Executive Director/Business
> and Legal Affairs, Dramatists Guild of America, Inc.

Playwrights should not interrogate whoever makes the initial offer or ask premature questions. They need to be mindful in all communications with the producer of how competitive the selection process is. A Reading can provide opportunities for development, exposure, or production. But before the writer makes a commitment, certain information should be entirely clear.

Before Accepting the Offer

1) Producers should inform playwrights of any type of attachment or restriction, such as an option, retainer, or right of first refusal.
2) The purpose and goal of the Reading should be identified. Institutions present Play Readings for a variety of reasons, and producers should be as forthright as possible about why they have chosen to present a Reading of this play and what they hope to accomplish.
3) Producers should specify the type of Reading they prefer and how much rehearsal time is offered. While Play Readings are most common, some producers prefer or require a Staged Reading or a Reading of a selection from the play. Some leave the decision to the playwright and director. Preferences or stipulations should be identified with the initial offer.

When an offer for a Reading comes from a professional or community theatre, most playwrights are eager to know the degree of interest in the play. While it is appropriate for a playwright to ask, they cannot always expect an answer. For many producers, the Reading will determine the extent of their interest.

> *At the Abingdon, we don't do development for development sake. Any play selected for a reading is a candidate for full production. But a reading is a date, not a marriage.*
> Kim T. Sharp, Literary Manager, Abingdon Theatre

While many theatres that present Play Readings have interest in the plays, in some cases there may be no chance for production. If so, the producer should state it directly. There are valid reasons for a playwright to accept an offer without the possibility of production. The producer may wish to begin an association with the writer, and the playwright may covet the chance to work with a creative team and develop a relationship with the theatre.

> *I usually suggest that my clients agree to an offer for a Play Reading. Readings are very often the first step in the formation of a relationship between a playwright and a theatre. Everyone wants to put one toe in the water and see how things go. Even if that particular play does not end up being developed, it can help create an atmosphere of trust and excitement about working together that can lead to other opportunities down the road. The main reason I might encourage them to turn down an offer is if the theatre is requiring some kind of "first refusal" to produce the play following a reading and the playwright is unsure of making that commitment.*
> Elaine Devlin, Agent

With this knowledge, playwrights can make an informed decision to accept or to decline the offer. They will know what is required of them and what the prospects might be for the play's future with the organization.

Playwright and Producer Discussion

Once the playwright accepts the offer, he or she should meet with the producer—in person, on Skype, or by telephone. It is vital for theatre artists to establish personal relationships. Email communications are not recommended. Even at festivals and other events where a large number of plays are chosen for Readings, personal contact between the producer and playwright is a worthy goal. Their first discussion is key in establishing a productive collaboration. Producers and playwrights become acquainted with one another, discuss the play, and establish a relationship based on mutual respect.

Institutions disseminate data in various ways. Producers should provide comprehensive information about the Reading that was not included with the initial offer as soon as possible.

Below is a list of questions playwrights might want to ask of producers. Not all of these questions apply to every Reading. Some may be more suited to labs or festivals than theatres. Playwrights should use their best judgment about which questions to ask and when to ask them.

Playwrights Ask Producers

- What is the exact date, time, and location of the Reading?
- What are the date, time, and location of the rehearsals, and is there flexibility?
- Is the play under consideration for production, or is it part of a Reading series with no chance of future production?
- Is there a possibility for additional developmental steps after the Reading?
- Will the producer expect or allow rewrites in advance of the Reading?
- If the playwright does not live in the city where the Reading is being held, will he or she be brought in at the theatre or organization's expense?
- Will housing be provided?
- If it is not possible to bring in the playwright, can they be Skyped in for auditions and rehearsals, or can they participate via cell phone?
- When is the final draft of the script needed?
- Is the organization presenting the Reading to interest theatres, universities, producers, or investors?
- Can the playwright continue to submit the play to other organizations?
- Can the playwright invite other producers to the Reading?
- Is a director attached? If not, will the playwright have input in the choice?
- Will the Reading be cast through offers or auditions, or will it be cast in advance without the playwright or director?
- If the Reading will be cast through auditions, where and when will they be held?
- Will the Reading be In-house or open to the public?
- Will the Reading be held in a rehearsal room or a theatre?
- What is the anticipated size of the audience?
- Who is the likely or intended audience?
- Is the playwright responsible for securing an audience?
- Will the Reading be followed by a talkback or a public response?
- Who will moderate the talkback, and is there a time limit?
- Will the playwright have a say in how the talkback is handled?
- Is a synopsis or any other materials required for marketing purposes?
- Is a character breakdown required?
- Will there be a follow-up discussion with the producer after the reading?
- Is there a possibility of a residency or commission?
- If the play is a finalist in a playwriting competition, is the winner chosen based on the play itself, on the Reading, or a combination of both?
- If the play is a finalist in a playwriting competition, what happens if it wins?

Securing a Director

After the initial communication between the playwright and producer, a director should be secured. A playwright needs a director who responds to the material and is eager to direct the Reading. At many theatres, playwrights suggest a director, often someone with whom they have a previous relationship or whose work they admire. The producer usually needs to approve the choice. Occasionally, playwrights will ask for suggestions or leave the decision entirely to the producer. A director should respond to an offer to direct a Reading promptly after reading the script.

At festivals and other organizations, directors are often assigned. Theses directors should have a genuine interest in the play and in directing the Reading before making a commitment. Assigned directors should arrange a discussion with the playwright after accepting the offer. When a director is assigned, a playwright has the right to challenge the decision if he or she feels the director is not suited to the project. Producers should support the playwright's decision.

Finding the Right Director

It's important for the director to care about the piece, to feel connected to it in some way. And it's also important that the writer and director have a long conversation about the work, about their communication styles, and about how they will work together. Writers can be very protective of their children. We need to feel like the script is in good hands, and that the director will honor the story, and hopefully make it better. Writers should come to an understanding with their director. If you can't be open and honest, then you'll hold back your opinions and build up resentments.

Mashuq Deen, Playwright; Actor

The director is there to help playwrights hear their characters, the intentions, to shape the rhythm of the piece. In their conversations with the playwright, directors should ask what the writer wants them to listen for.

Hayley Finn, Director

I must be involved in the choice of the director and the cast. When I was starting out, I had two experiences in which a theater wouldn't let me work with the director I wanted to work with—or very strongly suggested a director I didn't know. It's hard to resist these things when you don't have a lot of leverage, which a lot of young playwrights don't have, but in one of the instances, the theater made a great choice, and I'm thankful for their pushing me. In the other instance, the theater (and I) made the wrong decision in hiring someone. My advice would be, if a director you don't know is being strongly encouraged by the theater, a playwright should sit down with the director and get to know them as well as possible, with specific questions about the director's process and the play itself. If you have any misgivings, go back to the producers and explain your misgivings. There's always another option.

Rajiv Joseph, Playwright

Faculty directors are assigned in advance of the KCACT Festival. The Vice-Chair matches directors with playwrights, based on subject

matter and personal judgment, which works well. They are encouraged to talk to each other well before the festival.
Nancy Lee-Painter, KCACTF National Playwriting
Program Chair, Region 7

Generally, I like to see a director's work before hiring them. But sometimes, we'll hire someone "on faith." If actors or writers say they loved working with a director, that's a plus.
James Morgan, Producing Director,
York Theatre Company

Playwrights should choose directors based on a common understanding of what the play is. But they should be open to what the collaborator can bring to it.
Ralph Sevush, Esq., Executive Director/Business
and Legal Affairs, Dramatists Guild of America, Inc.

Selecting a director must be done with care and sensitivity, and the playwright's preferences should be respected. Some minority writers feel strongly that their work should be directed by someone who shares their ethnicity. Many women or LGBTQ writers feel similarly, particularly if their work deals with themes related to gender or sexuality. Other minority writers have no preference as to whether the play is directed by someone who shares their race, gender, or sexual orientation.

The best approach to securing a director for a play is to consult the playwright first. While situations exist where honoring the playwright's request is not possible, every effort should be made to do so.

Information for the Director

Before accepting the offer, a director should examine the protocols that were provided to the writer. Since their responsibilities differ, directors may require further information about the Reading. Below is a list of additional questions a director might ask a producer. Again, not all of the questions apply to every circumstance. Directors should use their best judgment in deciding which questions to ask.

Directors Ask Producers

- Are there preferences or policies about the type of Reading the producer wants?
- Who is the contact person before the Reading and during rehearsal?
- Will a stage manager, line producer, or coordinator assist with the responsibilities?
- Will the rehearsals be held in the same space where the Reading will be performed?
- Is it possible to rehearse outside of the allotted rehearsal time, in another space?

- What is the size of the venue?
- What are the dimensions of the playing area?
- Is the venue seating raked (on an upward incline)?
- Will the Reading be presented on a stage where there is a set for a full production? If so, can the furniture be moved?
- Is it possible to attend a Reading or performance at the venue in advance of the Reading?
- Is it possible to make a "site visit" to the venue before the rehearsal?
- If a visit is not possible, can photographs of the venue be obtained?
- Are there time restrictions for setup and strike?
- What is the anticipated size of the audience?
- Is it possible to use light or sound cues?
- Are CDs or MP3s preferred?
- Should the sound cues be sent in advance or brought to rehearsal?
- Is preshow music a possibility?
- Will there be body mics, enhancement mics, music stand mics, or no amplification?
- Will one-sided, three-hole-punched hard copies of the scripts in binders be provided?
- Are music stands, stools, and chairs available for rehearsal and for the Reading?
- Are dressing rooms available for the actors?
- Are there restrictions or requirements about what the actors can wear?
- Are there any union requirements?
- Will there be a printed program, and if so, what information is needed and when?
- Will there be a faculty advisor?
- Is there a stipend for the creative team?

The more information producers provide, the fewer questions playwrights and directors need to ask. If the information is not forthcoming or is incomplete, contacting the producer is necessary.

Guidelines

National New Play Network provides specific guidelines for the directors of the readings presented at our Annual Showcase of New Plays, but not hard-and-fast rules. We're open to thoughtful, considered adjustments in the guidelines, based on the needs of the play. We restrict blocking and limit production elements, but the directors control the look and feel of the reading, with the oversight of a line producer. With each Showcase, NNPN is going into a different community, so we want consistency from year to year and reading to reading.

Nan Barnett, Executive Director,
National New Play Network

There is an "assumption of knowledge" regarding how the readings are presented in KCACTF Region V. We prefer that the readings are clear and simple, and people who have been doing them a while know this, but there are no specific rules or guidelines for the readings.

Julie Mollenkamp, KCACTF National Playwriting
Program Chair, Region 5

At first, we didn't suggest policies for how readings were to be presented at Arcola, but it became clear that the more blocking or props, the less successful the readings. We tried to be hands off, but we learned that there is a best practice. Our guidelines grew out of trial and error. We prefer that actors are seated, with scripts-in-hand (in binders). They can stand to indicate they are present on stage, and some directors have had some success placing seats in different spaces of the stage to indicate location, but the other conventions remain the same. While the guidelines are still evolving, we're moving toward stipulating. But we're still testing.

Nick Connaughton, Creative Entertainment Manager,
Arcola Theatre

At Kennedy Center American College Theatre Festival Region VII, we prefer simple readings, at music stands. When directors did staged readings, it was harder to concentrate on the script, which is what we were evaluating. Most playwrights agree with this approach. We emphasize that we prefer this type of reading, but it's not stipulated, and sometimes, a little staging helps. The KCACTF National Playwriting Program is relatively new. Everything is evolving. It takes a while to see what works and what doesn't.

Nancy Lee-Painter, KCACTF National Playwriting
Program Vice-Chair, Region 7

Any theatre or organization that truly cares about supporting the playwright will provide guidelines to the directors, especially if those directors are guest artists and therefore not intimately familiar with the culture of the company. Several guidelines are dictated by the type of Equity contract the theatre is operating under. Additionally, each theatre or organization will have aesthetic guidelines, based primarily on the level of production support available and the knowledge of what their particular audience expects. The most important aesthetic guideline—and young directors often miss this—is to provide as clear and accessible a reading of the play as possible. The audience comes to Hear a play at a reading, so the mode of storytelling has to be adjusted for an Auditory experience rather than a Visual experience.

Jason Cannon, Associate Artist, Florida Studio Theatre

Playwrights and directors should compile their questions into as few emails as possible. Readings are only part of the programming at most institutions, and producers are involved with various projects. Responding to numerous email inquiries is time consuming, and something significant may be lost. Consolidating emails is a courtesy that helps to establish a healthy collaboration. This approach should continue throughout the pre-rehearsal process.

A stage manager, coordinator, or line producer may share the duties, allowing the director and playwright to focus on the presentation. When additional support is provided, most institutions have procedures for the distribution of responsibilities. However, in many cases, the playwright or the director is in charge of all aspects of the Reading.

CHAPTER 3

TIME RESTRICTIONS

Working within the time restrictions is the most significant challenge for the creative team involved with a Play Reading. While short rehearsal periods are common with many full productions, using time purposefully is mandatory with Play Readings.

Rewrites

Playwrights may make minor changes in the text during rehearsal for a Play Reading but not major rewrites. Submitting a work in need of substantial revision is a premature step that might compromise the play's future.

> *Some playwrights become unsure of themselves in development. Playwriting is not a science, it's an art. What if people said to Picasso, "Where is the nose!?" What if he heeded their advice? Some plays are read to death. I've seen plays where after years of development, the play was gone. It breaks my heart when I see a play get destroyed because the writer listened to everyone. I'm very conservative about giving an idea to a playwright. I don't think it's the actor's job. Writers shouldn't change a word until they see the actors on their feet. Actors and directors should never try to rewrite the script in rehearsals: "I think it would be better if. . . ." No no no! I tell the playwright, "Don't let them write your play! Take the advice you want, and throw away the rest. It's too long? It's called "A Long Day's Journey into Night." Simply, it is not my purpose to rewrite the play.*
>
> Lynn Cohen, Actor

Playwrights eager to make substantial rewrites after they receive a Reading offer should inform the producer. The offer is based on the submission, not on a substantially revised draft. After submitting the play, if a playwright feels a major revision is necessary, he or she should withdraw it from consideration.

Directors should not request rewrites unless there is an outright error in the script or unless the playwright and producer encourage this input. It can be a waste of time for playwrights to attempt to rewrite at the request of a director who may not be involved with the play in the future.

> *Rewrites should happen after the reading, not before—that's when true collaboration begins. Playwrights should not rewrite out of gratitude to the director.*
>
> Ralph Sevush, Esq. Executive Director/Business and Legal Affairs, Dramatists Guild of America, Inc.

Playwrights should use the Reading to discover possible revisions. Play Readings inform the rewriting process. Waiting until after the Reading to rewrite allows the creative team to use the rehearsal period to explore the current draft.

Playwright and Director Discussions

The playwright and director should discuss the play before rehearsals begin. As always, in-person discussions are best, but Skype or telephone conversations are effective alternatives. Email exchanges are less suitable for this type of exchange. There is no limit to the amount of time the playwright and director can spend on the play in the weeks preceding rehearsal, but at least one detailed discussion is necessary. Conversations between the playwright and director before rehearsal are one of the best ways to circumvent the time limitations.

> *While I like to talk to directors before rehearsals begin, these discussions are short. I prefer to talk about the play in rehearsal, in concrete ways. Then I'm sure we're on the same page.*
>
> Lauren Yee, Playwright

The playwright and director should establish a working relationship, particularly if they have not collaborated previously. A director may want to learn about the play's inspiration. A playwright may want to hear what the director admires about the work and answer any questions regarding tone, plot, character, and theme. The discussion should focus on the play and the Reading, not on a possible production. Significant scenes or beats that need to be foregrounded in the Reading, as well as anything that may present challenges, should be considered. They should also decide whether the playwright will communicate directly with the actors in rehearsal (which happens more often in Readings than full productions).

Playwrights should not be required to explain their work. While directors are free to ask writers to clarify aspects of the play, they should allow that certain writers may intend to be ambiguous. Some questions are better left unasked and unanswered. In more naturalistic plays, clarification of any confusion in the text is necessary, but directors should approach these discussions with the conviction that the play is unique and resist the temptation to turn it into something they have seen before.

> *I communicate with the playwrights via email until I get to the KCACT Region VII Festival, and then continue the discussions there. If I have any questions about the play, I ask in advance. I also ask playwrights what they most need to get out of hearing the*

play, and if there is any specific area they feel I could accentuate or explore in rehearsal for the reading. Sometimes the discussions are dramaturgical, especially if the play is dense or not immediately accessible on the first read. One particular play referenced ideas and concepts that I wanted to know a bit more about, so I did some research on my own before the KCACT Festival so I would feel more confident talking to the playwright. I have never requested rewrites.

Janet Gupton, Director; Professor, Linfield College

While some playwrights prefer involvement in every step of the process, others would rather hand over their play without discussion. This can be a useful way for writers to see if their intentions are communicated clearly in the text. However, this is the playwright's prerogative. A director should not decide unilaterally to rehearse the Reading without the approval of the playwright.

I encourage directors to ask questions. I try to initiate discussions. I make myself totally available. But some directors have no interest in talking. That's okay if you trust their aesthetic. But I'm suspicious when a director doesn't have any questions.

Caridad Svich, Playwright

Discussion can help the playwright and director see the play in fresh ways. Often, when artists communicate, putting thoughts into words kindles insights. Playwrights and directors can inspire one another. These early dialogues also allow the artists to explore and assess a collaborative relationship.

CHAPTER 4

━━━━━

CASTING

Casting policies vary within the institutions that present Play Readings. Playwrights, directors, producers, artistic directors, and festival coordinators may all participate. Playwrights should research casting procedures wherever they submit their work.

A casting director may be secured for Workshops or high-profile Readings.

> *We use a casting director on most projects at the York; it makes a big difference. We generally have a two-day open call for each Musical in Mufti, though sometimes we are able to get a concession from Equity that allows us to combine open calls for several shows. It's great when directors and writers have connections to performers, and we're open to ideas, but we can't pre-cast.*
>
> James Morgan, Producing Artistic Director,
> York Theatre Company

Character Breakdown

Playwrights who receive an offer for a Reading should generate a character breakdown if they have not already done so in the script. A character breakdown consists of a description of each character, including age, gender, occupation, physical characteristics, relationships to other characters, and personal qualities. While this information is likely evident when reading the script, a breakdown facilitates the casting process.

Breakdowns should be specific; analogy, metaphor, and comparisons to celebrity actors are best avoided. Also, playwrights should eliminate nonessential information. If a character's hair color is referenced in the play and has a specific purpose, it should be included in the breakdown. If it does not, it is unnecessary. Flexibility with age, gender, race, and physical type is encouraged whenever possible and can be noted in the breakdown.

Presented without scenery or technical enhancement, Readings allow for more flexibility with casting than full productions. Spoken stage directions can prevent confusion. If an actor in her forties is cast as a character in her sixties, the stage directions reader can reference the character's age. Without costumes to distinguish characters, if at all possible, actors should not play more than one role in Readings. If doubling is necessary, the stage directions reader can identify the character on each of this actor's appearances. For example, if an actor is doubling as Lisa and Bethany, the stage directions reader would say, *"Lisa opens the garage door"* and later, *"Bethany crawls through the window"* to avoid confusion.

At most theatres, the director and playwright usually cast the Reading. They consider actors they know personally or whose work they have seen and generate a short list of candidates for each role. Often, they ask colleagues for recommendations. In some cases, an actor may be asked to read a scene from the play with the director or someone on the literary staff, constituting an informal audition. But in most cases, actors do not audition for Play Readings; they are cast through offers.

> *Plays automatically become something else when actors are involved. You recognize the potential for different roles by seeing different actors perform them. You realize, "This role has got something." One of the things I enjoy most is actors who know how to take advantage of the "one-off" nature of a reading. Their instincts in the moment can be thrilling. One actor makes a strong choice, and the other actors can't fight it.*
> Ian Morgan, Associate Artistic Director, New Group

If the playwright lives in a different location than where the Reading will take place, the director generally assumes casting responsibilities. In addition to providing the breakdown, an out-of-town playwright should speak with the director to discuss how he or she envisions each character.

After obtaining contact information, the director or a representative of the theatre emails or telephones offers to the first-choice actors for each role. A description of the play and the character, and the day, time, and location of the rehearsals and the Reading should be included in the email. Offers should also inform actors of any compensation they will receive. Most actors will agree to be in a Reading without a stipend, but some remuneration, at least enough to cover transportation costs, is encouraged. Any requirements such as participation in a talkback, and any "perks" such as snacks or dinner, should be referenced in the email offer. If an actor finds it difficult to stand for long periods of time, he or she should let the director know that they will need to be seated for the Reading.

While attaching a copy of the play is not necessary, some actors request the script before accepting a role. When actors request a script, they should let the director know exactly when they will make a decision.

> *I ask to read a script before accepting an offer. Maybe it's a script that I'm not right for. I won't be able to help the play if I don't have a feel for it. There's no time in rehearsal to find that.*
> Lynn Cohen, Actor

Directors should not cast a Play Reading too far in advance. Most actors would rather be in a full production and will audition after they accept the offer. If they secure other work, they will withdraw. Approximately one month before the Reading is the best time to make offers, but an actor may pull out close to the performance date for a better opportunity. For this reason, a list of appropriate actors for each role and their contact information is important.

An actor who receives an offer should respond promptly. Generally, a director does not distribute simultaneous offers for the same role, and he or she is waiting to hear back before making another offer. If an actor is unavailable or uninterested, they should decline immediately. Actors who need a few days before making a commitment should indicate when they will know if they can participate. A quick response is an expected courtesy. If directors do not receive a reply in a few days, they can send actors an email reminder with a deadline.

If an actor is unable to participate after accepting an offer, he or she should let the director know immediately. An actor who drops outs of a Reading can suggest other actors and provide contact information. The director may not need these suggestions, but the gesture will be appreciated, particularly when the performance date is close.

Agents

While most actors in large cities have agents, it is accepted practice to contact actors directly with an offer. Many actors have websites that include contact information, and circumventing an agent is standard. Ultimately, actors decide whether or not to participate in a Reading without input from their agents.

> *Speaking for myself, I'm generally not involved at all in casting play readings. If there are particular roles that are hard to cast or if I have a strong suggestion, I would certainly offer it, but I tend to let the writer and director work that out together. It's perfectly fine for the director or playwright to contact actors directly, if there is a personal relationship, which there often is. I don't suggest stalking a beloved actor outside the stage door of their Broadway play. If they don't have contact information, it's appropriate for the director or writer to go through an agent, but try to be as specific as possible when making that contact. Are you making an offer for the actor to be in a reading at a specific theatre on a specific date, or are you inquiring as to general interest in the role?*
>
> Elaine Devlin, Agent

Celebrity Actors

Directors and playwrights who view Readings as opportunities to interest producers, investors, or theatres in their work may want to offer roles to well-known actors whom they envision in a full production. Many celebrity actors will participate in a Reading if it is being presented by an eminent theatre, if they admire the director's or playwright's work, or if the play and the role are of interest.

Before approaching name actors for a Play Reading, the director should weigh the options. While a celebrity actor may bring attention to a Reading and enhance the play's prospects, the balance of the ensemble might be disrupted. The audience may attend the Reading specifically to see that performer and not the play. Playwrights should know their goals for the Reading. As with a production, well-known actors should be approached when they are suited to the roles, not because of their status.

> *If you don't have the right actors, the reading won't represent the play's strengths. Casting a reading well is critical because there is*

so little time to rehearse, and you can't audition. Casting actors you've only seen on YouTube clips is a leap of faith, as is trying to cast "starry actors." Going to see plays, offering roles to actors within your orbit, and asking colleagues for advice are great ways to cast.

Daniella Topol, Director

Emerging Actors

Given their proliferation, Play Readings are an effective way for early-career actors to be seen by people in the industry. But because Readings are generally cast through offers, it can be difficult for emerging actors to participate. This creates a "Catch-22" situation. How do actors get a foot in the door in a theatre community where no one has seen their work?

Strategies for early-career actors are well covered, but the ways in which participating in Play Readings can play a part in career advancement are underexplored. While full productions are still cast by auditions, Readings increasingly serve as preliminary auditions for many plays. Young actors should consider ways to become involved.

Becoming Involved

- Attend as many Readings and productions as possible at theatres where you would like to work.
- When you attend, introduce yourself to the playwright, producer, literary manager, and director.
- Research whether you can send or email a headshot and résumé to the theatre or casting director. Readings are rarely cast from headshots and résumés, but these are useful follow-ups to an introduction.
- Send information about any Reading or production in which you are performing to producers, artistic directors, literary managers, and directors. If they do not attend, they may send a representative from the organization. These notifications inform them that you are working. If the show has been reviewed, include a quote. If your performance is singled out, that is the quote to pull. Be sure to invite people to projects that you are certain you want them to see.
- Volunteer to read stage directions for a Reading.
- Volunteer to be a "reader" at production auditions.
- Get your work seen in any venue. A performance at a comedy club, a fundraiser, or a concert can serve as an "audition."
- Look into internships.
- Volunteer to be an assistant or an observer on a Reading.
- Generate an audition reel. While clips from film appearances are useful, clips from stage productions are generally less so. The best way to create a reel is to film a few scenes or monologues that display your skills.
- Take classes at theatres where you are interested in working.

Casting at Labs, Theatre Festivals, and Other Organizations

When playwrights and directors are brought in from out of town, producers may assume complete casting responsibility either through offers or through a general audition held by the lab or other organization. These auditions often take place once a year and are open to all actors in the community. From these auditions, producers generate a group of performers suitable for upcoming developmental work. These producers are also familiar with the local acting pool and can draw from that.

Organizations such as The Kennedy Center American College Theater Festival, the National New Play Network, and the American Association of Community Theatre approach casting in various ways, even within the regions or theatres they represent. Some Readings are precast. Other Readings are cast through general auditions at the start of the festival or conference. Callbacks are often possible.

Festival Auditions

Auditions take up the whole first day of the KCACT Festival for the playwright and director. Most of the time, we're able to secure a good cast, but there are always a few actors that everyone seems to want—and the negotiations begin. Another challenge is when playwrights have written in very specific needs, such as identical twins! I let the playwright have the final say in casting.

Janet Gupton, Director; Professor, Linfield College

Casting at the Festival rather than at the schools where the playwright is from allows students from other schools that did not have a play selected to become involved with the National Playwriting Program.

Nancy Lee-Painter, KCACTF National Playwriting
Program Vice-Chair, Region 7

Assembling a strong cast is compulsory for an effective Play Reading. This can be achieved through open communication and the combined efforts of the creative team.

The casting process benefits when playwrights are involved. They know their work best and can offer valuable insights. Producers and directors will have their own casting ideas, and the organization may have specific procedures. Playwrights need to work within these policies and collaborate with the director and anyone else involved with casting. But unless they prefer not to be included, playwrights' voices should be heard.

I'm good at casting. Usually in a reading situation, especially if I am in a city where I do know local actors, producers let me cast. I have an eye for who is good for my stories— which actors can inhabit the space, texture and language. I have an ear for the overall "music" of the piece, so I like an actor with a high reedy voice next to one with a low voice. I like actors who make smart, deep, unexpected choices. With auditions, you can figure out if they don't connect with the work. With readings, you don't have that luxury. Actors in a reading are putting themselves out there.

Caridad Svich, Playwright

CHAPTER 5

MODEL FOR A PLAY READING

Most theatre artists agree that for a standard public Play Reading, simpler is better. But "simple" means different things to different people. Various approaches exist. All have value. The only rule is that a Reading should serve the goals of the playwright and the needs of the play at that particular point in its development.

Simplicity

Some producers, directors, and playwrights prefer Play Readings that are basic and unadorned. In these Readings, actors often do not look up from their scripts or attempt to connect with their fellow actors. They are usually seated in chairs and do not change locations during the Reading. Actors hold the scripts in their hands or place them on their laps and do not physicalize their characters in any way.

This approach has advantages, particularly in the early stages of a play's development. The pace and rhythm of the play are consistently maintained. There are no unnecessary pauses and no risk of paraphrasing. Actors are unencumbered with movement and physicality, allowing for complete concentration on the text.

In Favor of Simplicity

Emotionally or technically complex plays benefit if the actors are seated. There are lots of elements, and being seated allows the actors to focus, and relate to each other. Standing requires them to consider the audience, and give their characters a physical life. This can stand in the way of hearing the play.

Ian Morgan, Associate Artistic Director,
New Group

A line of music stands can feel like a barricade, and makes it difficult to have a sense of intimacy at a reading.

Daniella Topol, Director

Actors in a reading shouldn't disengage with the text in an effort to engage with the other actors. It is terrific to engage, but you have to make sure that you are reading what is written and not engaging with someone at the expense of the text.

Lisa Rothe, Director

Good readings are very simply presented, with the focus on the text. Less successful readings often incorporate too many elements of staging that distract from the text. We found many actors looked uncomfortable when they had blocking, props and the text to juggle. And music stands impose a visual barrier. If actors are wandering around with props and trying to remember blocking, you can't listen to the play which is the primary purpose of a reading.

Nick Connaughton, Creative Entertainment
Manager, Arcola Theatre

Too much movement in a reading can destroy the piece. Actors are reading the script, and being forced to concentrate on blocking makes it more difficult for them to read the lines the way the authors' intend. And any attempt to look up and down and make eye contact in a reading alters the rhythm and pacing of the play. Even a micro-second can have an adverse impact, especially with a comedy. If the point it to create a pause, that's fine. But the actors in a Reading should only interact with the dialogue, not their fellow actors. They are reading the role, not acting the role. Most Readings allow just enough rehearsal time to read the role, not perform it. The challenge is that everyone wants to bring the play up to performance level. Directors should work with the actors on character intentions, not blocking.

Ralph Sevush, Esq., Executive
Director/Business and Legal Affairs,
Dramatists Guild of America, Inc.

Simpler is better. I think readings are most effective when actors are actually reading with simple staging. Stick with the words. With too much action, actors paraphrase, which is not right.

Lynn Cohen, Actor

When a Reading is presented this way, the limited rehearsal time is devoted exclusively to investigating the script. This can be invaluable to playwrights. But while these Readings can be useful as explorations, they are often less effective as presentations.

If actors do not look up from their scripts or connect with their fellow actors, audiences will hear the words, but the character relationships may be diluted.

And if actors do not change positions or physicalize their characters, the play may be more difficult for audiences to access.

Enhancement

Certain theatre artists prefer more creative Readings. The difference may be as slight as a conceptual arrangement of the music stands. Or the Reading can incorporate staging and production elements. Even with limited rehearsals, more experienced directors can find inventive ways to present Readings. This approach can help producers, directors, playwrights, and audiences envision the full production.

In Favor of Enhancement

I am fascinated by what makes a reading work well, and being able to direct a reading is an important skill for directors involved in new work. Directors need playwrights to have careers. Most directors are capable of shaping the emotional contours and intellectual arguments of the play in a reading, which can provide a genuine experience of having the play unfold. But it's lovely when directors take the next step, unleashing some of their own point of view. Readings should not be a rote experience.

James Bundy, Dean/Artistic Director,
Yale School of Drama/Yale Repertory Theatre

My first time directing at the KCACT Festival, I had a lot of ideas about concept and staging, such as breaking up one of the roles into different voices since this character was not seen onstage. I was very satisfied with what the playwright and I accomplished. Since he had already seen a performance of the play, it was fun to experiment, and he was very open to exploring other directions that the play could go. But the Festival guidelines stress that the readings should be simple. I feel that sometimes, by asking for such minimalism, they stifle any creativity that may serve the reading of the piece.

Janet Gupton, Director; Professor,
Linfield College

Once you develop your skills, you can do more interesting things. There's no right way. What is the "set" as communicated by the music stands? A play about loneliness might benefit from one music stand, center stage, separated from the other music stands. Every piece dictates something different. Maybe you choose one moment to shift, to move, to transform the music stands. They can be raised or lowered to suggest driving a car or writing at a desk. Or someone stands on a chair. Or the actors turn their pages in unison. How do you suggest simply that an actor is in a bathtub? A rug on the floor becomes a playing area. The central thematic point of the play should determine the style of the reading.

Jose Zayas, Director

But even in the hands of experienced directors, the effort to enhance a Reading may turn clumsy, and the result can resemble an under-rehearsed production. An actor's focus is compromised if he or she is required to give too much thought to movement and physicalization—let alone costumes and props—with little rehearsal time and an unmemorized script. When actors are distracted from the text, the presentation is weakened rather than enhanced.

A director is essential for coordinating all of the elements necessary for a quality Reading, but many theatre artists feel that directors who use a Reading as a creative opportunity for themselves do a disservice to the writers. They argue that concept comes later in a play's journey. Directors can use Readings to discover what those concepts might be.

Play Readings benefit most from directors' interpretive and organizational skills. But even with limited rehearsals, there are ways in which the creative team can make genuine artistic contributions. Given that the number of Play Readings continues to grow, it behooves all theatre artists to have a clear sense of how Readings can be presented with maximum impact and effectiveness.

The Model

The model considered throughout this book strikes a balance between simplicity and enhancement. Most Play Readings presented by professional and amateur theatres, labs, and other organizations use a similar approach. While the model may seem prescriptive, the guidelines should be modified and tailored to accommodate the play, the playwright, the venue, and the event.

The Proposed Model for a Play Reading

- *Actors are seated or standing behind music stands, which hold the scripts.*
- *Actors manipulate the music stands so they can read the script and relate to their fellow actors easily.*
- *Actors look up from the script at their fellow actors.*
- *Actors and directors determine moments of direct eye contact.*
- *Actors physicalize their characters and convey the intention of eliminated and spoken stage directions.*
- *Directors determine music stand positions for the actors in each scene in the play and, often, for moves within certain scenes (internal moves).*
- *Stage directions are edited, revised, and relocated.*

In the model, actors performing in a scene are positioned behind music stands—standing or seated on stools or chairs. Actors not performing in a scene are seated nearby. No official nomenclature exists to describe where actors who are not in the scene are positioned. The term "retreat positions" is used in this book. Actors move from retreat positions to specific music stands in ways that correspond to the plays' dramatic intentions and the characters' motivations. The moves and compositions can result in effective presentations.

With small-cast plays, determining the movement in advance is not required. But with large-cast plays, directors should enter rehearsal with a clear plan for movement. While nowhere near as detailed as the staging for a full production—even basic directing terminology such as blocking does not apply—the simple, visually revealing moves that benefit Play Readings are best determined in advance.

When to Block

I don't write down blocking in advance. Entrances and exits are like math, and the playwright has already created the math. I make quick blocking choices in rehearsal. Learn about the play, and make choices as you're watching rehearsal with the playwright.

Jose Zayas, Director

There is usually very little rehearsal for a reading, so the director must do 90% of his/her work before rehearsals start. This means all blocking (minimal as it is), all tech (if allowed), all cuts (of stage directions), and the big picture emotional choices must all be completed prior to rehearsals. If that stuff is happening during your limited hours of rehearsal, then you aren't prepared, you aren't serving the play or the playwright, and the actors will not have the chance to go at all beneath the surface. Readings are not a place for "organic" directing, there simply isn't time. And it all goes back to the philosophical reason for readings: to let the playwright hear their play as clearly as possible. It is quickly apparent if a director of a reading is in it for their own sake rather than the sake of the playwright. Basically, in a reading the director needs to be more of a technician than an interpretive artist. Show off the play, not your directing skills.

Jason Cannon, Associate Artist,
Florida Studio Theatre

Some rules of thumb for readings: 1) Limit discussion in rehearsal. There's a point at which discussion ceases to be useful. By discussing too much, you're opening doors that you can't walk through with the limited time you have. There's no time for real table-work, so it's okay to be result-oriented. 2) Decide on the purpose of the reading. 3) And don't stage it. When you stage a reading, you're only learning how to stage a reading. 4) Also, in advance of your rehearsal,

> *plan which stage directions you'd like to hear, and notate this in the script given to the actors. It's a huge rehearsal-time-swallower to choose stage directions to read; don't waste precious time. 5) And always have food!!*
>
> Adam Greenfield, Associate Artistic Director,
> Playwrights Horizons

The Venue

Ideally, the director is able to visit the venue before rehearsal. Attending a Reading or full production at the venue gives directors first-hand knowledge of how the space—whether it is a rehearsal room, an auditorium, or a theatre—will affect the Reading. A site visit without attending a performance is also worthwhile.

If visiting the venue is not possible, directors should request the following: links to photographs, the exact dimensions of the stage or playing area, the size of the house, whether the stage and/or the seating are raked (a term that refers to an upward incline), the seating arrangement (proscenium, thrust, or other), and the distance from the front edge of the playing area to the first row of the audience.

Proscenium seating, with the entire audience facing the actors directly, is optimal, as "opening up" to an audience seated on three sides is difficult for actors reading from scripts. Audiences should be able to see the actors from head to toe in a Reading. To achieve this, the seating should be raked, the playing area should be raised, or the actors should stand when they are in a scene. If thrust seating is stipulated, seating is not raked, and the playing area is on the same level as the seating, directors should know in advance and determine the best placement for the actors.

Often, rehearsals are held in a different space than where the Reading will take place. Preferably, the rehearsal room is not smaller than the playing area in the venue. Readings are occasionally presented on a "dark night" at a theatre where a full production is running. Directors should ask if the furniture or any other set pieces can be removed or moved upstage so that the Reading can be performed in an open playing area downstage.

Music Stands

A music stand is a device used by musicians to hold their scores. They are now standard equipment for many Play Readings. Music stands should be sturdy, with a solid "desk" (the upper part of the music stand, where the script rests) and a tripod at the bottom with legs close to the floor (see Photograph 5.1). Flimsy, lightweight music stands should not be used for Readings: They are difficult to manipulate, and scripts can easily tumble off.

The best rationale for using music stands is that they free actors' hands. Holding a script limits an actor's ability to physicalize a character. And while holding scripts allows actors more freedom of movement than when positioned behind music stands, for audiences at a public Play Reading, the sight of actors walking about script-in-hand can look like they are rehearsing. A Reading should not evoke a rehearsal. If directors decide against music stands, actors should be seated.

Whether or not to use music stands and how to arrange and manipulate them will affect the style and quality of the presentation.

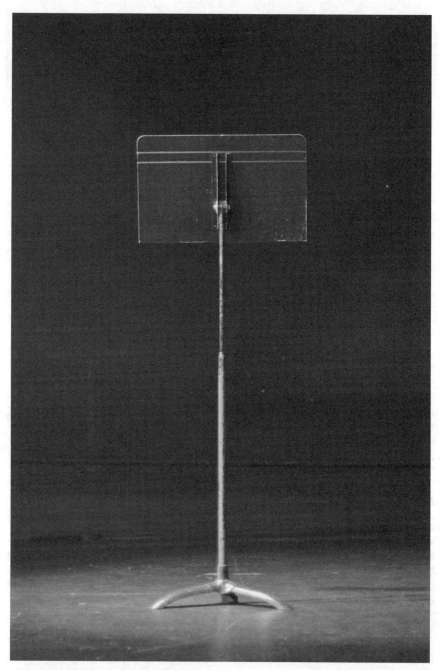

Photograph 5.1

Views on Music Stands

I appreciate when directors use the concept of actors standing at music stands in an active way—using different depths, different playing areas, angling and adjusting the music stands—and doing all this within a limited rehearsal period. But readings are less successful when they are bogged down by too much presentation, with costumes, props and actual staging that you don't need to efficiently tell the story.

Lauren Yee, Playwright

In some instances music stands are fine. They provide a kind of formality if that is what you are after. In my opinion, they can form a kind of barrier. Sometimes when an actor holds a script it frees up their relationship to the audience. Binders are more rigid but are sometimes necessary. It all depends on the personality of the play and the event for which it is being staged. Once, in a play about Salvador Dali, I had the actors toss their pages away when they had finished reading them. It created a chaos that only an artist could truly appreciate.

David Esbjornsen, Director

I love music stands. They become like a part of my body.

Susan Louise O'Connor, Actor

Number and Placement

The number and placement of music stands for a Reading is determined by the director before rehearsal, which can be done efficiently with information about the venue and familiarity with the script. To determine how many stands are required, a director locates the scene in the play with the largest number of actors. Each actor in this scene will need a music stand, as will the stage directions reader.

The playing area should be large enough to accommodate all of the music stands. Plays with large casts need larger playing areas. The stands should be at least one foot apart, or further apart if the stage is larger and a greater distance suits the play. Actors should be able to gesture without hitting each other.

In most cases, the distance between the music stands should be uniform, but stands can be placed in seemingly random positions. Or one music stand can be separated from the others, giving it prominence—whatever best serves the play.

With large-cast plays, when music stands are placed in a straight line, it is difficult for actors to look up from the script and make eye contact (see Photograph 5.2). Arranging music stands in a semicircle, with the center of the semicircle upstage, permits actors to interact with actors who are not next to them.

The placement of the music stands in relation to the audience must be precise. These positions are determined by the height of the stage, the slope of the seating

Photograph 5.2

rake, and the distance from the first row of the audience to the stage. If audiences are too close to the stands, they will not see the actors' faces. Directors or stage managers should use spike marks (a placement marker, usually tape, on the floor of the stage) when the positions for music stands have been finalized in case the stands are accidently moved.

Directors should check sightlines when arranging the semicircle to be certain that the audience seated on the sides of the venue can see the actors' faces, particularly the two at the downstage ends. In small-cast plays, a semicircle is not necessary.

Height and Numbering

The height of a music stand, which may need to be adjusted by every actor who uses it, should be positioned so that the actor does not have to look too far down to read the script. If music stands are too low, audiences will have a better view of the top of the actors' heads (see Photograph 5.3). If the stand is too high, part of the actor's face will be blocked (see Photograph 5.4).

One of the three legs of the tripod at the bottom of the music stand should be pointed directly upstage. Actors use one foot to hold the music stand in place while lifting the desk with their hands. Placing one of the tripod legs directly upstage facilitates this (see Photographs 5.5 and 5.6).

Preferably, the music stands do not have lettering stenciled on the side that faces the audience. "Property of the Music Department" is not something that the audience should be required to see throughout the Reading. Music stands should be numbered on the upstage side of the desk, from the actors' perspective—stage left to stage right. Numbers can be placed on the floor upstage of each music stand. Any type of tape can be used for this purpose provided the numbers are clear.

Angling

When music stands are facing directly out and actors attempt to look at each other, the actors will need to look down to read their lines and then look up and turn their heads to see the actor they are addressing (see Photograph 5.7). If one of the actors angles her music stand, she will be able to read the script and then look up at her fellow actor. If the other actor's music stand is not angled, she will need to look down at her script to read her lines, then look up and turn her head (see Photograph 5.8). When both music stands are angled, actors can read their lines and then look at up at their fellow actors easily. Actors experienced with Readings will often angle their music stands instinctively (see Photograph 5.9).

There may be interpretive or stylistic reasons why actors in certain plays or certain scenes should not angle their music stands and face directly out. Directors can determine in advance which plays or scenes benefit when actors angle their music stands and which do not.

Actors should use caution when angling music stands. If a music stand is angled perpendicular to the other actor, the speaking actor will be in profile.

If there are three actors in the scene, the actors stage left and stage right can angle their music stands. The actor center stage can keep his music stand straight out. This arrangement allows all three actors to look down at their scripts and look up at their fellow actors easily (see Photograph 5.10).

Quality music stands are essential for quality Readings. Actors should be able to raise and lower them without difficulty and adjust the angles so the

Photograph 5.3

Photograph 5.4

Photograph 5.5

Photograph 5.6

Photograph 5.7

Photograph 5.8

Photograph 5.9

Photograph 5.10

desks can be turned easily from side to side. Music stands should not be moved from their positions on the floor when manipulated, nor should they be picked up and relocated during a Reading unless the move is purposeful. Actors look awkward when lugging music stands across the stage. Music stands that require effort to raise or lower or that slip down after they have been raised can harm a Reading.

Theatres, labs, and other organizations should not skimp: They need a sufficient number of sturdy, adaptable music stands on hand for large-cast Readings. Also, given the specified placement and manipulation of music stands and the movement of actors, music stands should be available for the entire rehearsal period.

The assignments of actors to specific music stands for each scene, and the adjustments of the stands made by actors create revealing movement and compositions for a Play Readings. These simple techniques enhance the experience of the presentation for the audience.

Standing or Sitting

In addition to determining the number and placement of the music stands, directors must decide whether the actors will be standing, sitting on stools, sitting on chairs, or variations of these options. The decision is informed by the demands of the script, the specifics of the venue, and, at times, the ages and body types of the actors.

Standing provides actors with the most effective means to physically inhabit the characters, even if the character is meant to be sitting. A spoken stage direction will let the audience know whether the character is standing or sitting if this information is necessary.

When actors are standing, every part of their body can communicate character. The physical choices should be natural and instinctive, not studied and deliberate. In most cases, how actors embody their characters is left to the actors. They should not be encumbered with too much directed physicality.

> *Gestures have to be fully motivated or they will look false. If the actors can't achieve that, don't ask them to do it.*
>
> Nick Corley, Director; Actor

Stools

Sitting on stools is a viable option to standing. Again, directors should consider the script, the venue, and the cast when making this choice. Stools compel actors to keep their bodies alert and let them make character-specific physical adjustments.

Music stands should not be too high or too low when actors are seated on stools (see Photograph 5.11). When music stands are angled and are at the correct height, actors on stools can use their bodies to reveal character and can easily connect with their fellow actors (see Photograph 5.12).

As with music stands, stools and chairs should be strong and sturdy. Wobbly or noisy stools or chairs, like flimsy music stands, should be avoided for Play Readings (see Photograph 5.13).

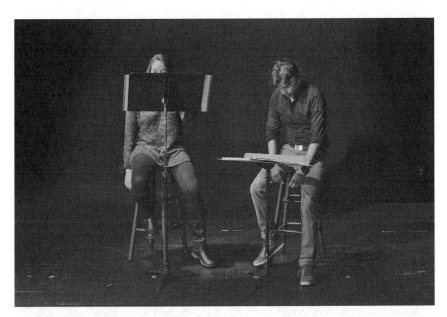

Photograph 5.11

Photograph 5.12

Photograph 5.13

Chairs

In intimate venues, or in settings where the seating would make it difficult for the audience to see actors standing or perched on stools, sitting in chairs can be the best choice. Again, music stands must be positioned properly (see Photograph 5.14).

However, it is challenging for actors to make physical adjustments with minimal rehearsal time when sitting in chairs, reading from scripts. They should be reminded to keep their bodies attentive and alert (see Photograph 5.15).

If space allows, directors can add a few additional chairs. This permits an actor to move to another chair during the Reading. But these moves should be limited. If a director prefers to change the actors' positions more than a few times, the actors should be standing.

When actors in large-cast plays are seated, they will likely need to play certain scenes with actors not seated next to them, looking across actors who are not in the scene. In these cases, the actors seated between the actors in the scene should look down at the scripts. A clear visual convention must be established and maintained when actors are seated to avoid confusion.

Additional factors that impact the choice of standing, sitting on stools, or sitting in chairs are the age and body types of the cast. Standing or sitting on stools for over two hours can be physically demanding. For Readings that are cast with large or elderly actors, sitting in chairs is often the most considerate choice (see Photographs 5.16 and 5.17).

Alternating between standing, sitting on stools, and sitting on chairs can be interpretively revealing. But whatever the choice, in the proposed model, the scripts should be placed on music stands. And whether the actors are standing or seated, it is important for the stands to be the proper height so audiences can see their entire bodies. Often, when actors are seated for a Reading, there is no need for "Retreat Positions," as discussed below. They can simply stand and adjust their music stands when they are in the scene.

Retreat Positions

Retreat positions are chairs located upstage of the music stands or, if the playing area is not deep enough, off left and right. Reading conventions allow these actors to be seen by the audience throughout (although if a character's appearance in the play is meant to be a surprise, that actor can be offstage). When actors are in retreat positions, they should be seated at a distance from the actors performing in the scenes so they can enter and exit with ease. They should have enough light to read their scripts but preferably not the same intensity of light as the actors performing in the scene. Retreat position chairs should be identical unless the script supports another choice.

When in retreat positions, actors should hold the script in their laps, and focus on their scripts and not on the actors performing in the scene. If they react to the performing actors, they function as audience surrogates. A physical distance between the actors at music stands and the actors in retreat positions helps to establish a visual vocabulary that tells the audience who is in the scene and who is not.

The maximum number of actors who are not in a scene determines the minimum number of chairs in retreat positions. For example, if there are never fewer than four characters in a scene in a six-character play, at least two chairs in retreat

Photograph 5.14

Photograph 5.15

Photograph 5.16

Photograph 5.17

positions are required. If directors prefer the actors to be seated in retreat positions when the play begins or after each scene, the number of chairs is determined by the size of the cast.

Retreat position chairs should be in a straight line. These actors do not need to look at each other, and a straight line conveys a visual contrast with the semicircular arrangement of music stands for actors performing in the scene.

While each music stand should be numbered so that actors can be assigned to a specific stand for each scene and for any internal moves, numbering the retreat position chairs is usually not necessary. Actors will determine retreat positions themselves, and in small-cast plays, they return to the chair under which they have stored their bottles of water.

With large-cast plays, actors should retreat to the chair closest to their exit or to the chair closest to the music stand for their next entrance. A few extra chairs in retreat positions can make access easier when there are more than a few actors. With some large-cast plays, the director can number the chairs and assign actors to specific retreat positions. The number of music stands and the number of retreat position chairs should be determined before rehearsal begins.

Placement of Stage Directions Reader

The stage directions reader's music stand should be at a distance from the actors' stands but not in a retreat position. The best placement is left or right of the semicircle of music stands and further from the other stands than they are from each other. While music stands for the characters in a scene are often angled in a semicircle, the stand for the stage directions reader should face out. Readers are not characters, and placing the readers outside of the semicircle and a few feet from the nearest music stand communicates this compositionally. Also, if the actors are standing, the reader could be seated on a stool. If the actors are on stools, the reader could be in a chair like those in retreat positions. Directors should find a way to distinguish this person from the characters in the play.

Diagrams

Once directors determine the number of music stands that will be placed on the stage, the number of chairs in retreat positions, and the placement of the stage directions reader, they should generate a diagram. Directors can create and print out template diagrams for the play on a computer and insert copies between the pages of the script where characters enter, exit, or move to other music stands, just as directors insert ground plans of the set in their scripts for productions. For our purposes, we will use a scene from "Under the Mango Tree," a play with six characters (see Diagram 5.1 and Appendix G).

Directors can also hand-draw a template diagram for the play, print out copies, and insert them in to the script (see Diagram 5.2). Or they can simply sketch diagrams opposite any page near lines where characters enter, exit, or make internal moves, as in the examples below. For this reason, and also because actors often use the opposite pages for notes, one-sided scripts are best for Readings.

Characters in the Diagram

For simplification, in the diagrams, each character can be indicated by the first letter of their name, or the first two letters if more than one character's name begins with the

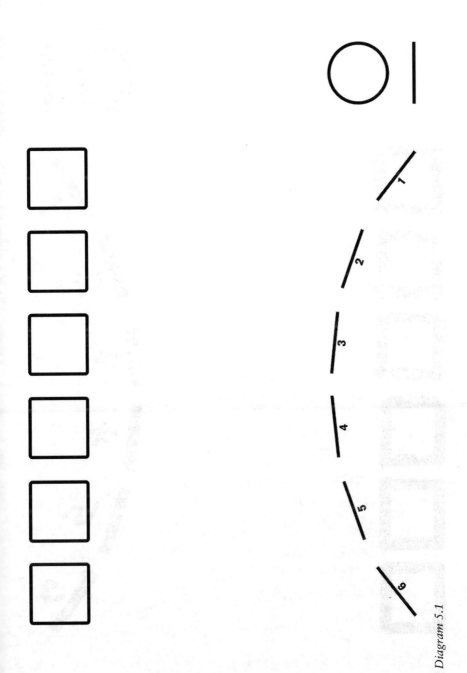

Diagram 5.1

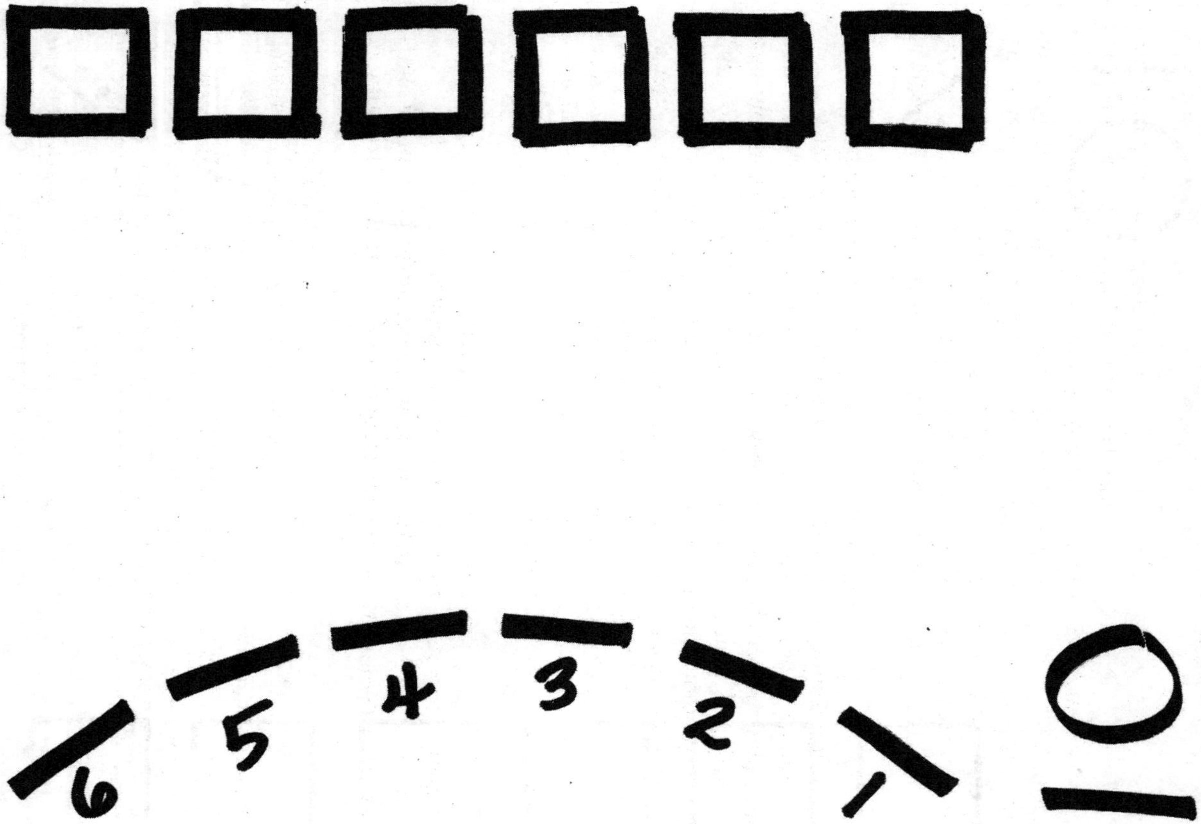

Diagram 5.2

same letter. In "Under the Mango Tree," the characters' names are Lena, Fela, Gloria, Belan, Junior, and Felix. In the diagrams, they are referred to as L, F, G, B, J, and Fx.

There are six characters, so the Reading will need at least seven music stands, which includes one for the reader. An examination of "Under the Mango Tree" reveals that the play contains scenes where the stage is empty, which means at least six chairs are needed in retreat positions. The minimum numbers are therefore seven music stands, six chairs, and one stool for the stage directions reader. If the director chooses to have the actors seated on stools or chairs, then six additional stools or chairs would be required.

Additional Chairs and Music Stands

While a Reading of "Under the Mango Tree" could be presented with seven music stands, in certain scenes all of the characters are onstage. The director might include an additional music stand, which provides possibilities for internal moves, as discussed below. An extra chair in retreat position is also helpful for plays with more than a few characters. There are now eight music stands, seven chairs in retreat positions, and one stool. These requirements should be communicated to the producer in advance so that the necessary equipment is available when rehearsal begins (see Diagram 5.3).

Placement and Movement of Actors

If the director has decided that all the actors are in retreat positions before the Reading begins, they can be assigned to chairs closest to their music stand positions for the first scene. Or the director could decide to begin the Reading with the actors in the first scene at their assigned music stands. The director should also decide whether the actors return to retreat positions after each scene or move directly to their music stand positions for the next scene. For our purposes, let us assume that the director prefers the actors to return to retreat positions after each scene (see Diagram 5.4).

> SCENE 3
> TIME: EARLY MORNING
> *Lights slowly fade up. Fela enters with a bowl and*
> *a bag. She sits down with bowl on her lap.*

Based on a study of the scene, the director has determined that Fela will move to music stand 6 (MS6). An arrow is used to convey this move (see Diagram 5.5). In rehearsal, the director will inform the actor playing Fela that she will be positioned at MS6. Directors and actors should use pencils to make notations in the diagrams and scripts, as changes are likely.

> FELA Lena . . . when you finish talking to your
>   mother, come outside.
> *Fela begins cutting open beanstalks. Lena enters*
>   *upset.*

The director has determined that Lena will move to MS5 (see Diagram 5.6). These positions and moves are indicated in director's script, either on the inserted printout of the diagram or the hand-drawn diagram on the facing page.

Diagram 5.6 indicates that Lena and Fela are standing next to each other. Since the stage directions state that Lena is *"upset"* when she enters, perhaps the

Diagram 5.3

Diagram 5.4

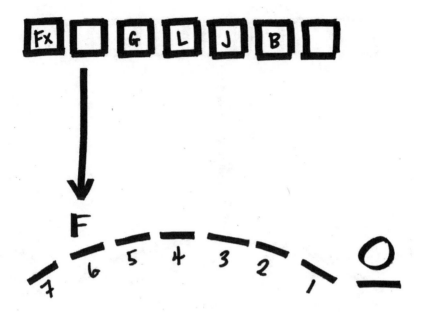

Diagram 5.5

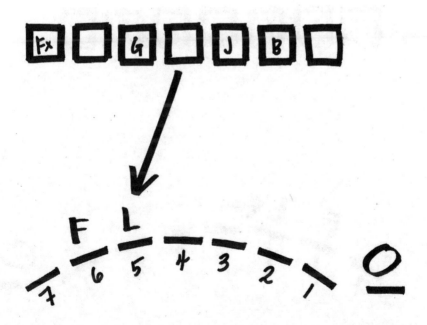

Diagram 5.6

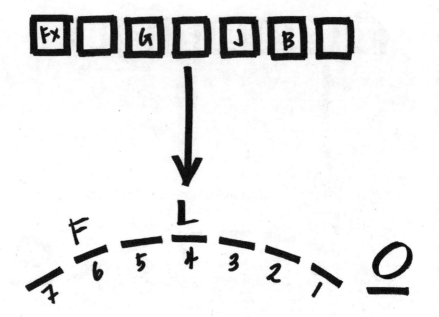

Diagram 5.7

Diagram 5.8

director decides she should not be next to Fela. In that case, Lena is at MS4, leaving an empty music stand between the two actors (see Diagram 5.7).

FELA What did your mother say?
LENA Nothing.
FELA What do you mean nothing?
LENA Nothing . . . you were the one who wanted me
    to talk to her so I did.
FELA You should want to talk to your mother.
LENA She doesn't say anything. She just asks me—
    are you okay? Are you behaving?

The director may decide it is useful for Lena to move to the music stand next to Fela for the line, "She doesn't say anything" (see Diagram 5.8).

Clear, simple moves such as this can convey to the audience in visual terms that a character's motivation is shifting. This is how movement for a Reading works. Though not as detailed as blocking or staging for a production, it serves a similar function, which is to communicate dramatic intentions visually.

The director may decide that the actor playing Lena can angle her music stand toward Fela, and the actor playing Fela can make the same adjustment. These modifications also suggest a shift in the characters' objectives (see Diagram 5.9).

Multi-Character Scenes

While Scene Three from "Under the Mango Tree" involves only two characters, many of the scenes include additional characters, requiring more decisions about placement and movement. (See Appendix G.) However, the same principles apply.

One of the most common challenges with large-cast plays is that over the course of a scene, various characters address each other. In a full production, the scene would be blocked so that these characters move closer to the characters they are addressing. In a Play Reading, attempting to move actors next to each character they address in a multi-character scene consumes rehearsal time. Directors should decide on the best single placement for the actors in such scenes and then determine any moves within the scene.

A careful read of the play reveals which characters should be standing near or next to each other. Directors can also decide which, if any, characters should not be near each other and which characters' placement is most flexible. Given that the music stands are in a semicircle, actors can easily address any other actor.

During the scene, if it is useful for an actor who needed to be near one character to move next to another character, this actor can relocate to the unattended music stand. In determining the single best placements for this scene, the director should decide how the unattended music stand can be used for internal moves. More than one music stand can be added, but the decision should be made before rehearsal. These moves should be limited, and directors should avoid requiring actors to cross behind other actors too often when changing positions.

In the final scene from "Under the Mango Tree," all six characters are onstage. To determine the best placement for the actors in this scene as well as any internal moves, the director reviews the stage directions for specified action. Having examined the entire play, the director knows which relationships and dramatic events

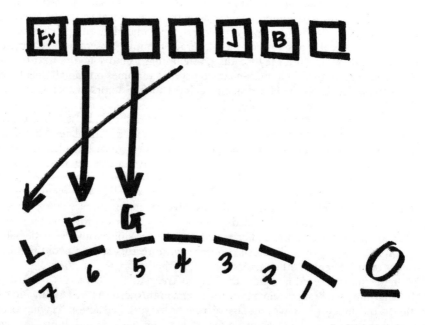

Diagram 5.9

Diagram 5.10

are most significant. This informs which characters should be near or next to each other at various points in this scene and, importantly, for the final moment. When the scene begins, all actors are in retreat positions (see Diagram 5.4).

```
SCENE 18
TIME: ONE WEEK LATER—LATE AFTERNOON
Gloria enters with a dress in her hand.
GLORIA Hello I am here! It's Gloria . . . Hello
    . . . Is ANYBODY home?!
Fela enters in her Sunday best.
FELA Hi Gloria.
GLORIA I brought something for Lena. I hope she
    likes it.
FELA Lena, there's someone here to see you. LENA!!
Lena enters patio.
GLORIA Hi Lena.
LENA Hey.
GLORIA The dress is for you Lena—for the Fiesta of
    San Lorenzo.
LENA No way.
FELA You have to go the Fiesta, like a young lady.
LENA Ah man . . .
GLORIA I made it for you.
LENA/FELA What?
FELA Let me see.
Fela checks out dress.
```

Three characters are now onstage. The stage directions suggest that Fela would be near or next to Gloria so she can *"check out"* the dress. Based on this, the director should make a preliminary indication in pencil of the entrances of the three characters and their placement at specific music stands (see Diagram 5.10).

While the diagram might suggest a "traffic problem," Lena enters after Gloria and Fela. Notice that the stage directions do not specify whether Fela takes the dress from Gloria or just looks at it. The director will make a decision informed by other considerations in the scene, as discussed below.

```
GLORIA It's my first "GLORIA"!
LENA You made it . . . my first dress, now I gotta
    wear it.
GLORIA You better.
Felix enters—he brings flowers with him.
FELIX Hola . . .
FELA Hola Felix.
FELIX Thank you for inviting me. For you.
He gives her the flowers.
FELA Thank you. They're beautiful . . . I'm so
    sorry, I didn't mean to . . .
```

```
FELIX Don't say anything.
LENA I forgot something inside . . . um . . . let
    me bring the flowers inside . . .
Lena exits back into the house.
```

At this point in the scene, a few actions have occurred that would inform the positioning of the actors. Felix has entered and gives flowers to Fela, suggesting he should be next to her. But in the director's previous positioning, there is no music stand next to Fela. The diagram should be revised to reflect a different position for the actors, allowing Felix to be next to Fela. The stage directions state that Lena takes the flowers back into the house, so she should also be near or next to Fela. While Fela should be near Gloria to *"check out"* the dress before Felix enters, she does not need to be next to her to do so (see Diagram 5.11).

With this positioning, Felix can enter and give the flowers to Fela, and Lena can take the flowers from her. With large-cast plays, adapting and adjusting to find the best possible position for actors in each scene is one of the director's most significant pre-rehearsal responsibilities.

```
LENA Gloria . . . come on . . .
GLORIA But . . .
LENA Would you come on already! Help me put on my
    dress!
GLORIA Stop bossing me around.
LENA You're the one that likes to boss people
    around.
They both exit into house.
```

The stage direction implies that Lena moves from her music stand to a retreat position. The move would tell the audience that she has left the patio. But the character has more lines, so she should not move just yet. Instead, she could take a step back, away from the music stand, suggesting that she is starting to exit. The move is useful but not essential (see Diagram 5.12).

Returning to a previous consideration, if Fela took the dress from Gloria when she *"checked it out,"* she must have handed it back, as Gloria has the dress when she exits. **How the actors will make this clear to the audience is discussed in Part Two.**

Fela is at MS6, and Felix is at MS5. They are next to each other and alone onstage, suggesting a romantic interest. They should remain next to each other through the end of the play to reinforce their attraction (see Diagram 5.13).

Notice that Lena and Gloria are in different retreat positions than earlier. During the scene, Lena was positioned at MS7, so sitting in a retreat position further stage right makes her exit easier. Also, when these two characters return, Gloria enters first, so there will be no traffic problem.

```
FELIX You look beautiful. Oh . . . I have
    something else for you.
Felix gives Fela a mango.
FELA A mango?
FELIX Strangest thing . . . You know we couldn't
    chop down the tree? Some demolition specialist
```

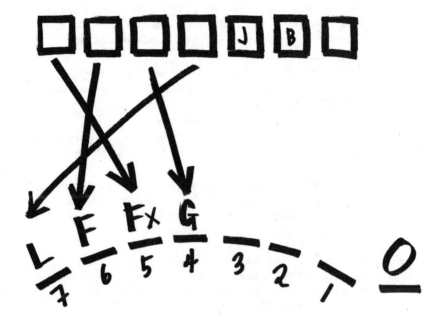

Diagram 5.11

Diagram 5.12

> comes over—he hits the tree—the axe nicks it.
> He tells us the tree is alive. And sure enough
> the mangoes are fresh. Can you believe it?
> FELA Fresh? . . . Life is . . . sometimes . . .
> very strange . . .
> FELIX Telling me—couldn't cut down the tree so I
> finally had to pay off the Diaz family so that
> I could lay down the water pipe.
> *Fela smells mango as Belen enters.*
> BELEN Look at how handsome my grand . . . oye where
> are you? Junior get over here right now!!
> Junior.
> *Junior enters dressed in an elegant "white guaya-*
> *bera." It is a dress shirt commonly used in*
> *the Caribbean—with four pockets on the front*
> *of the shirt.*

Belen and Junior enter. The director determines the best placement for these characters based on actions specified in the stage directions, including the re-entrance of Gloria and Lena, which occurs soon. Lena is the main character in the play and should be center stage when it ends.

Belen enters before Junior. She could move to MS3, near Felix and Fela, but she would need to relocate soon to make room for Lena and Gloria. Thus, the best position for Belen and Junior is stage left. Belen gives her grandson Junior "a nuggy," so they should be next to each other when they enter. Looking ahead, Junior should be near or next to Lena at the end of the play. If Belen is assigned to MS1, when Junior enters he can take MS2, which would leave MS3 and MS4 available for Lena and Gloria. Felix compliments Junior on his appearance but does not need to be next to him (see Diagram 5.14).

> JUNIOR I feel stupid.
> BELEN Mira que handsome. I felt bad about punish-
> ing him so much so I bought him all these new
> clothes and a new basketball. He's teaching me
> to play. Verdad . . .
> *Belen gives him a nuggy.*
> JUNIOR Yeah, whatever.
> FELIX Junior you look like a young man.
> JUNIOR Thanks, I guess.
> BELEN Fela, I'm glad you called . . .
> FELA Sh, sh—mija, you're like my sister, I'm sorry.
> BELEN Esta bien.

Fela and Belen reconcile. Should Junior and Felix hear these lines? A study of the script provides the best answer. For our purposes, suppose the playwright or director prefers the moment to be private. In production, Belen would likely approach Fela, but that would be too much movement for two lines in a Play Reading. Simpler solutions exist.

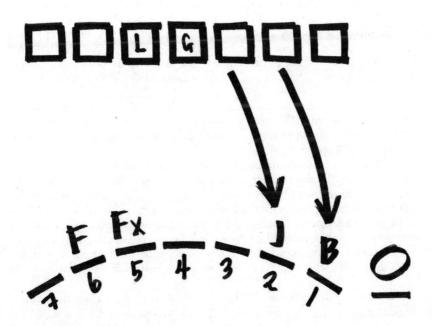

Diagram 5.13

Diagram 5.14

Private moments in multi-character scenes can be achieved simply if the speaking actors angle their music stands toward each other and the nonspeaking actors take a step upstage from their music stands and look at each other. This is easier than continuously moving actors to different stands. Directors should be selective, and move actors to other music stands within scenes only when necessary. Felix and Junior should not return to retreat positions, as they have not exited the scene (see Diagram 5.15). They could also turn and face upstage, but that type of move is formal and only suited to certain plays.

> FELA . . . Lena, Lena, Gloria , let's go . . .
> *Gloria enters.*
> GLORIA Attention everyone . . . Lena will be modeling an original "Gloria."
> *Lena enters with dress on, but she still wears her sneakers.*
> BELEN Oye, look how beautiful you two are. Lena, you're wearing a dress.
> LENA Oh brother.
> GLORIA We have to work on her footwear—pero the dress looks good huh?
> JUNIOR Hi Lena.
> FELA We're all ready. Let's go.

Lena and Gloria enter. This is the first time anyone has seen Lena in a dress. Junior, who has previously called Lena a tomboy, admires her new look. His line "Hi Lena" hints that he sees Lena as a girl for the first time. As referenced above, Lena and Junior should be near each other at the end of the play. This would mean that Gloria moves to MS4 and Lena to MS3 (see Diagram 5.16).

This positioning would work, but a better option exists. If Fela and Felix were to move stage right to MS7 and MS6 when Lena enters, there would be three unattended music stands center stage. These actors could justify this move; they want to get a better look at Lena. If Gloria takes MS5 and Lena takes MS4, MS3 is unattended (see Diagram 5.17).

With these positions, when Junior says, "Hi Lena," he could move from MS2 to MS3, next to Lena. The move is stronger than if he were already there. It is the type of simple adjustment that can have a great impact, particularly at the end of the play (see Diagram 5.18).

As this discussion illustrates, directors should allow time before rehearsal to examine the entire play scene by scene to determine the music stand positions and the internal moves for the actors that best convey relationships and events. This can be a satisfying process for the director and can reveal the play in simple visual terms to the audience. Choices and compromises are necessary to avoid too much movement. Directors should be discerning; not every beat in a Play Reading can be articulated through movement. But when directors do their pre-rehearsal work conscientiously, actors can focus on their performances in rehearsal.

> *It can be a wonderful challenge to find simple yet evocative staging that conjures the action described by the playwright. And with minimal rehearsal time, you can call forth the world of the play in a revelatory way.*

Will Pomerantz, Director

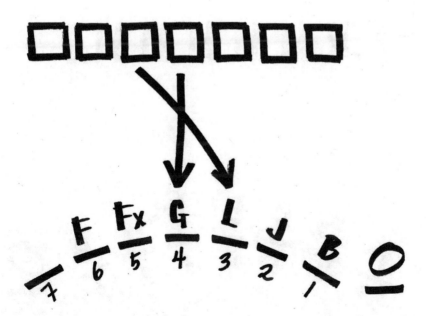

Diagram 5.15

Diagram 5.16

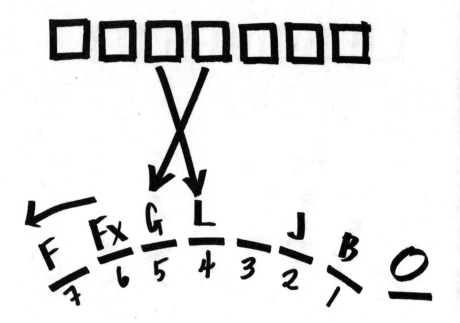

Diagram 5.17

Diagram 5.18

Clothing, Hair, and Makeup

In informal Play Readings, actors can wear "street clothes"—that is, what they would normally wear—as long as the clothing is neat and does not contain text, logos, or images. But this can result in a wide range of styles, which may be confusing to audiences. Directors can ask actors to wear "stage blacks" or something dark, which will give the cast a unified look. They can also suggest that actors wear "character-appropriate" clothing. This is fine for contemporary work but more difficult with a period play. Directors should be ready to offer ideas about what kind of character-appropriate clothing they have in mind if they suggest it. Whatever the choice, the director should decide in advance, and the actors should be notified so they can bring the proper attire to rehearsal. Actors should not be required to buy anything for a Reading.

Nor should they be asked to make any major adjustments to their hair or facial hair. For most Readings, hair color and length do not matter. Spoken stage directions can clarify any significant differences between the actors' personal appearance and the characters'. But if an actor's hair is dyed an unusual hair color or his or her head is shaved, they should inform the director when they receive the offer. Actors with long hair can be asked to put their hair up or keep it down. They can also start with their hair up and let it down at an interpretively revealing moment. Actors generally do not need stage makeup for a Reading.

CHAPTER 6

STAGE DIRECTIONS

Traditional stage directions are written by the playwright to inform readers of time period, set considerations, production requirements, stage action, blocking, entrances and exits, line interpretations, and, in some cases, the style and tone of the play. They offer guidance and inspiration to the creative team and are not written to be spoken aloud in a full production. Stage directions are formatted differently from the dialogue, usually in italics and often in parentheses. No uniform rules exist about how to write or format stage directions. Playwrights should write their stage directions and format their plays however they like.

> *Playwrights shouldn't be expected to follow any rules about formatting or stage directions. The way a writer chooses to lay a play out on the page is, for me, a big insight into the tone and sensibility of the play. There are so many different ways a play can look, or read. How it looks best on the page, from the perspective of the person who wrote it, is a clue to me about how to interpret their work. There are no rules. Nuanced, revelatory stage directions are fine. There is no way that things have to be.*
>
> Adam Greenfield, Associate Artistic Director,
> Playwrights Horizons

Playwrights approach stage directions in various ways. Some favor detail. George Bernard Shaw's lengthy stage directions read like essays. Other writers describe blocking extensively. Some playwrights specify how certain lines should be interpreted by placing an adverb before a line of dialogue such as *"adoringly"* or *"suspiciously."* Harold Pinter is notorious for stipulating every pause actors should take between lines. Many playwrights write novelistic, poetic, or unconventional stage directions, which pose challenges for Readings.

> *The function of my stage directions is to give actors clues to the tone of the play, and to convey a sense of the play's personality and flavor. Sometimes, I write "emotional" stage directions—images that aren't intended to be literal or production-specific. For example, when I wrote "A tumbleweed rolls by," I didn't intend for a tumbleweed to roll across the stage—my intention*

was for the actor and director to convey loneliness and isolation.
In a production, you won't see a tumbleweed (at least, I hope you
won't!), but the stage direction gives you a sense of the world.
Lauren Yee, Playwright

Many writers prefer spare stage directions written in a direct voice, distinct from the tone of the dialogue. Some playwrights write their stage directions with great care, while others are less conscientious.

Historically, stage directions in published scripts were taken from the stage manager's prompt book. Currently, the quantity, content, style, and formatting of stage directions in published plays are the playwrights' prerogative, with occasional input from the publisher.

It's up to the playwright how they want their stage directions to
appear. Our editorial philosophy is very "hands off" in terms of for-
matting. The only real requirement is that there's some way for the
reader to differentiate between the spoken dialogue and the stage
directions. Occasionally, we will proof the stage directions to be
sure that they're clear, for example, if a character begins to speak,
at some point earlier, the stage directions should indicate that this
character entered. Playwrights need to be sure that their vision
translates—that the published version stands alone as a production
guide. If there are challenges related to staging a show, we encour-
age author's notes, instead of extensive, instructive stage directions.
Character descriptions are totally up to the writers, though
detailed character descriptions are beneficial for producers, as well
as directors and actors. It is important for Playwrights to under-
stand how stage directions help their play work on the page.
Amy Rose Marsh, Literary Manager, Samuel French, Inc.

Publishers, unions, guilds, and agents prohibit any cuts or revisions to be made to the text of a published play. They also require that no stage direction is eliminated in a Reading of a published work without permission from the playwright. However, they do not require directors to follow the stage directions as written.

In a full production, some directors heed every stage direction. Others ignore them entirely, going so far as to eliminate the stage directions before rehearsals begin. However, important information is often included in stage directions, and a willful disregard of the playwright's intentions is ill-advised. A reasonable compromise exists. Directors should read and consider all stage directions and try to understand the playwright's objectives. They are then free to use whatever stage directions support their approach to the work and disregard those that do not.

Stage Directions for Readings

Certain stage directions need to be read aloud in Play Readings to provide audiences with information that would be evident in full productions. Therefore, the cast for most Readings includes a person charged with this task.

Stage directions are edited for Readings unless they are particularly sparse. Some playwrights or directors do this at rehearsal collaboratively with the actors.

When to Edit

Before a reading, I'll take a quick pass at which stage directions should be cut, but I prefer to cut them in the room, with the director and actors.
Caridad Svich, Playwright

Editing the stage directions has to happen in rehearsal, on instinct, with the participation of the actors and playwrights.
Ian Morgan, Associate Artistic Director, New Group

I don't edit stage directions in advance. I listen to them in rehearsal, figure out which ones are valuable to help create a rhythm for the play, then check with the playwright, and make a decision on the spot.
Jose Zayas, Director

This can be effective for plays with very few stage directions. But in most cases, an edit of the stage directions completed in advance will save rehearsal time, a precious commodity with Play Readings.

Ideally, directors and playwrights collaborate on the edit. Either can generate a first draft of the edits, then adapt and adjust through discussion. Stage directions can also be relocated, revised, or rewritten by the playwright or by the director with the writer's approval.

Playwrights who have had numerous Readings often limit the number of stage directions in their plays to facilitate the editing process. Writing stage directions with any consideration toward what would be easier for Readings is unnecessary.

Certain directors feel that they are violating the writers' intentions by editing a single stage direction. But stage directions are not written to be heard; they are suggestions for the creative team, and most playwrights do not write stage directions with a sense of how they will sound and how they will impact the flow of the play when read aloud.

Why Edit

Some writers see stage directions as an opportunity for creativity. They see them as integral to the production of a play, and it can be hard to give them up for a reading. But their inclusion can sometimes be a problem for the audience, interrupting the flow of the action or the rhythm of the storytelling.
Nan Barnett, Executive Director, National New Play Network

We strongly advise directors to determine which stage directions to read, without input from the playwright. The playwright will (understandably!) usually feel protective and want more stage directions read than are necessary or advisable.
Jason Cannon, Associate Artist, Florida Studio Theatre

In a full production, the information in the stage directions is revealed to the audience through design, action, and performance. While some of this is necessary for the audience at a Play Reading, much of it is not. Whenever a stage direction is spoken, the audience's focus is taken from the actors. Stage directions that are numerous or lengthy can weaken the Reading. The goal is to eliminate as many stage directions as possible but never at the expense of clarity.

Given the considerable variations in the quantity, quality, and style of stage directions, editing must be done conscientiously. There are few standardized rules. Some suggestions and examples are provided below.

Editing Stage Directions

The first step in editing stage directions is to examine the play thoroughly before making any cuts. This is the only way to determine which information is required for an understanding of the play.

The title of the play and the playwright's name are the first stage directions the audience hears in a Reading. In most cases, act and scene numbers are also read, although this is not essential, and should be considered on a play-by-play basis.

The Setting

Many plays begin with a lengthy description of the setting. Below is the set description for "Death by Design." (See Appendix G.)

> Scene: Cookham, England. 1932. The living room of
> the country home of Edward and Sorel Bennett.
> The room is decorated with comfortable
> furniture including a sofa with pillows, a
> small end table with a drawer, a few chairs
> and lamps, and a carpet. The front door is
> Down Right. French windows are Upstage,
> leading to a garden. A staircase Up Left
> ascends to the bedrooms, and Edward's study.
> There is a service door beneath the stairway
> leading to the kitchen, and to the root
> cellar. Paintings, a mirror and a clock adorn
> the walls. Also in the room are a bookcase,
> a gramophone, a closet or hat rack, and a
> bar trolley with liquor, glasses and an ice
> bucket.

While useful for directors and designers, not all of this information is necessary for Reading audiences. Here is the stage direction, revised and edited.

> Scene: Cookham, England. 1932. The living room
> of a country home. The room is decorated
> with comfortable furniture. In the room are
> a front door, a staircase, a service door
> beneath the stairway and French windows

```
leading to a garden. Paintings and a mirror
adorn the walls. Also in the room are a
bookcase, a gramophone, a hat rack, and a bar
trolley with an ice bucket.
```

How would the director and/or playwright arrive at this edit? Below are the questions they should consider. While the process may seem painstaking, with knowledge of the play, editing a setting description can be accomplished in a few minutes.

1. Does the audience need to know who owns the country home? If it becomes evident in the play, the phrase *"of Edward and Sorel Bennett"* can be cut. If this phrase is eliminated, the stage direction should be rewritten; the word *"the"* would be changed to *"a,"* so it reads, *"The living room of a country home."*

2. Should the audience hear about all of the furniture and props in the room? A careful study of the play discloses that the phrase *"including a sofa with pillows, a small end table with a drawer, a few chairs and lamps, and a carpet"* is not necessary.

3. It is best to eliminate any theatre-specific jargon from stage directions as such terms may be unfamiliar to a general audience. They are suggestions, not requisites; there is no need to force audiences to envision a specific environment. Also, revising the stage directions here is advisable. The sentences *"The front door is Down Right. French windows are Upstage, leading to a garden. A staircase Up Left ascends to the bedrooms, and Edward's study. There is a service door beneath the stairway leading to the kitchen, and to the root cellar"* can be adapted to read as follows: *"In the room are a front door, French windows leading to a garden, a staircase which ascends to the bedrooms and Edward's study, and a service door beneath the stairway leading to the kitchen, and to the root cellar."* This eliminates all theatre terminology.

   Note that if the phrase *"of Edward and Sorel Bennett,"* is cut, audiences may be confused to hear that the stairway leads to *"Edward's study."* An edited stage direction often has repercussions. If *"Edward's study"* is eliminated, it begs the following question:

4. Should the audience know at the beginning of the play where the stairs and French windows lead? If it is not important, or will be revealed through dialogue or a later stage direction, these "destination" phrases can be eliminated. This part of the stage direction would then read, *"In the room are a front door, French windows, a staircase, and a service door beneath the stairway."*

5. With the above cuts, specifically *"leading to a garden,"* the audience would not know that the French windows are actually doors (often, they are referred to as French doors), which a study of the play reveals is pertinent. Perhaps this has been too extensively edited, and part of the stage direction can be restored: *"In the room are a front door, French windows leading to a garden, a staircase, and a service door beneath the stairway."*

6. This edit might suggest to the audience that the French windows lead not only to the garden but to the staircase and a service door beneath the stairway. Revising the sentence so it reads, *"In the room are a front door,*

a staircase, a service door beneath the stairway and French windows leading to a garden" eliminates any confusion.

7. To determine which furniture, set dressing, and props the audience should hear about, each needs to be examined separately: *"Paintings, a mirror and a clock adorn the walls. Also in the room are a bookcase, a gramophone, a closet or hat rack, and a bar trolley with liquor, glasses and an ice bucket."* The paintings, the bookcase, the gramophone, the closet or hat rack, the mirror, and the bar trolley have important functions in the play, so they should be maintained. But most bar trolleys contain liquor, glasses, and an ice bucket. Should these items be edited? The ice bucket has a distinct function in the play. Thus, the liquor and glasses can be eliminated but not the ice bucket.

8. Lastly, while the director and the designer may appreciate options for where the characters hang their coats, audiences do not need to hear about both, so *"a closet or"* can be cut.

Based on the above considerations, here again is the stage direction for the description of the setting, revised for the Play Reading:

> Scene: Cookham, England. 1932. The living room
>   of a country home. The room is decorated
>   with comfortable furniture. In the room are
>   a front door, a staircase, a service door
>   beneath the stairway and French windows
>   leading to a garden. Paintings and a mirror
>   adorn the walls. Also in the room are a
>   bookcase, a gramophone, a hat rack, and a bar
>   trolley with an ice bucket.

This may seem a laborious task, but spoken stage directions influence the audience's experience of a Play Reading. If they are lengthy or convoluted, they disrupt the flow of the presentation. Stage directions should provide necessary information in a concise manner. They can be rewritten, if need be, so they are easily spoken and understood. Carefully edited stage directions guide the audience through the Reading and allow them to focus on the actors.

Reading Draft

After carefully editing the stage directions, playwrights or directors can generate a Reading draft, with the pre-rehearsal edits indicated by "strikethrough" (a typographical function which places a horizontal line through edited text, allowing the text to remain visible). Struck-through Reading drafts allow the cast to see the playwright's intentions and permit an edited stage direction to be reinstated in rehearsal.

The Reading draft should be emailed to the actors and stage directions reader. Without a Reading draft, actors spend rehearsal time transcribing the edited stage directions into their scripts.

Directors should request that hard copies of the script are available for the artistic team when they arrive for rehearsal. The scripts should be three-hole punched and in binders. Binders prevent loose pages from falling to the floor.

Binder clips or brass fasteners are acceptable, if not ideal substitutes. A slightly larger than standard font size that allows actors to read the text more easily can be useful, particularly for plays with roles for elderly performers.

Stage Directions Reader

Directors should cast an actor to read stage directions, or at least an individual with a strong speaking voice and stage presence. When stage directions are assigned to someone without these qualities, the audience can lose important information.

Reader Requirements

A stage directions reader should lead the way, but not give it away.
Lauren Yee, Playwright

Stage Directions Readers shouldn't hide. They're part of the event, not a side-bar. They're guiding the story at the same level as the actors. I like when directors read stage directions. They know the work well, and will give it the right energy.
Caridad Svich, Playwright

We insist on the director casting an actor or acting intern as the reader of stage directions, someone who is entirely comfortable performing in front of an audience. Too often this job is overlooked and falls to an assistant stage manager or literary intern, which isn't fair to them or to the play. How the stage directions are read makes a huge difference in the quality of the Auditory experience for the audience, which then directly impacts how much the playwright can glean from the reading. When directors do not stay within the guidelines, the reading suffers from a lack of clarity, the playwright doesn't learn as much, and the audience is far less able to provide useful feedback.
Jason Cannon, Associate Artist, Florida Studio Theatre

While the reader should assist in establishing and maintaining the tone and tempo of the play, in most cases, the reader should not "act." In a production, this person would not be onstage. They should resist any temptation to insert a character into the play that does not exist.

Hiring an actor to do stage directions who is determined to make the reading about them can lead to problems. Each stage direction becomes an opportunity to emote and milk moments, which is as problematic as a flat delivery. Fortunately, this is rare.
Will Pomerantz, Director

Stage directions can also be divided among the actors in the cast, particularly with large-cast plays. This should be done only to serve the play and not to parcel out opportunities for actors with smaller roles. When stage directions are distributed among the cast, to avoid confusion, an actor reading stage directions for a specific scene should not be a character in that scene. Nor should actors read stage directions that apply to the character they are portraying. For example, if the stage directions state that a character *"sits and reads the newspaper,"* that actor should not be given that stage direction. This device calls attention to itself and makes it challenging for the actors to stay in character.

Props

Deciding which stage directions to edit for Play Readings involves a consideration of properties, commonly known as "props." Props pose problems for Play Readings. Even with scripts on music stands, actors need their hands to turn pages. This is difficult when holding a prop. Also, a table would be needed nearby to store props, as resting them on music stands is risky.

A stage direction may read *"Mary hands Elaine a letter."* While a letter would be easy to handle in a Play Reading, what if Mary hands Elaine a bouquet? Or a Ming vase?

Incorporating props into Readings takes time. Actors must rehearse how they are handled. Props also fight Reading conventions. Given that they are performed without scenery or costumes, Play Readings do not require props.

Stage directions that identify pertinent props should be retained. This lets audiences visualize the props when they hear the stage directions. Mary does not need to hand Elaine a letter if the stage direction *"Mary hands Elaine a letter"* is read while, simultaneously, the actor executes a gesture that suggests the action. **What actors do when stage directions are read is discussed in detail in Part Two.**

That said, a certain prop might serve a significant function in a play. For example, if a scarf is used to strangle someone, the director may choose to add this prop to the Reading. If the scarf can be incorporated efficiently, it might provide just the right flourish. But no prop is essential for a Reading.

Adverbs

Playwrights often write adverbs in parentheses preceding specific lines of dialogue to suggest delivery. For example, a playwright might write *"(anxiously)* Why did you come here?" They also include adverbs within longer stage directions, as in *(He paces around the room, anxiously awaiting her arrival).* Certain playwrights employ instructional adverbs extensively. Some of the directives are critical, for example, *"(flirtatiously)* Why did you come here?" is quite different from *"(anxiously)* Why did you come here?" But many are optional. Either way, audiences do not need to hear them. Actors and directors are capable of conveying playwrights' intentions. Redundancy aside, it is rather silly to hear the stage direction reader say, *"anxiously,"* and then have the actor deliver his line in an anxious manner.

Along with adverbs that precede lines of dialogue, eliminating adverbs in internal stage directions is also useful. *"Daniela, enraged, picks up the vase and furiously hurls it at his head"* is more effective without the adverbs: *"Daniela picks up the vase and hurls it at his head."* The actor portraying Daniela will supply the rage and fury. If *"enraged"* and *"furiously"* are read, the actor is forced to impersonate described behavior.

Consistency

Spoken stage directions should be clear, coherent, and consistent. Conventions should be established and maintained. If an early stage direction reads, *"Ben opens the door,"* then all stage directions should include the pronoun. If the director chooses to have the reader say *"Opens the door,"* then pronouns should be eliminated throughout. If the choice is, *"Opens door,"* then all stage directions should be read without pronouns and articles. However, while a sentence fragment such as *"opens door"* might be an effective choice for certain plays, stage directions are easier for audiences to understand if they are complete sentences. Fragments are appropriate for stage directions in a script, but in a Play Reading, they should usually be rewritten as complete sentences.

In certain cases, the director must decide between a character's proper name and a pronoun. If the stage directions are *"opens door,"* then *"walks into the room,"* then *"hides in closet,"* they should be revised to read, *"Ben opens the door,"* *"He walks into the room,"* and *"He hides in the closet."*

There are other considerations involved in editing stage directions. Although the preliminary edits should be made before rehearsal, as many of these choices concern the placement, movement, and physicality of actors for the Reading, the discussion will continue in Part Two.

A Review of Pre-rehearsal Responsibilities

- A playwright has accepted the offer from a producer for a Play Reading, and they have discussed what the offer entails.
- A director has been secured and has discussed the play with the writer.
- The Reading has been cast, including the stage directions reader, who will attend all of the rehearsals, along with the entire cast. "Staggered rehearsals," where actors arrive at different times, are not ideal for Play Readings.
- Unless the director has decided to edit the stage directions in rehearsal, a struck-through Reading draft has been emailed to the actors and stage directions reader.
- The number of copies of the Reading draft needed for the artistic team has been communicated to the producer or stage manager.
- The director has requested that the Reading drafts are three-hole punched, in black binders, and printed on one side of the page. A larger font size may also have been requested.
- The director has sent the producer or stage manager the required number of music stands, stools, and chairs, including those for retreat positions, and requested that these items are in the venue or rehearsal room when rehearsal begins.
- If the Reading will have a stage manager or line producer, the distribution of responsibilities on the day of the Reading has been discussed.
- The director determines how the rehearsal time will be used.
- In diagrams in the Reading draft, the director has notated the placement of the music stands and the positions and movements of the actors.
- Directors may note when the actors angle their music stands, look up from their scripts, and make eye contact.

- If directors are unfamiliar with the venue, they have visited the site or requested photographs and dimensions of the playing area.
- Everyone involved in the Reading has been sent a reminder of the rehearsal schedule and directions to the venue.
- The playwright, director, and cast have been informed of any compensation they will receive and when they will receive it.
- The director has told the actors what he or she would like them to wear for the Reading.
- Any additional information that might be useful to the actors such as whether they will be required to participate in a talkback, whether there are vending machines in the venue or restaurants and convenience stores nearby, and when the cast will break for dinner has also been provided.
- The actors have emailed the director specific questions about the script.
- Actors have been given the director or stage manager's cell phone number in case of any emergency.

PART 2

REHEARSAL AND PERFORMANCE

CHAPTER 7

BEFORE REHEARSAL BEGINS

The Director and the Stage Manager

On the day of rehearsal, if access to the venue is possible, the director arrives before the actors and meets with stage manager or line producer. Having discussed the distribution of responsibilities, they prepare the room. If there is no stage manager, the director assumes the day-of-rehearsal tasks. The playwright can assist.

The playing area should be cleared. Flats, masking drapes, abandoned scripts, and other extraneous items should be removed. Nothing should distract the audience's focus from the actors. The playing area may need to be swept or mopped. The room temperature should be comfortable.

The director sees that all the requested materials are on hand: the exact number of hard copies of the script in binders and the correct number of chairs, stools, and music stands. All of the stands should be checked for sturdiness and flexibility. If any of the music stands cannot be raised or lowered easily or do not stay in place when raised, they should be replaced. If that is not possible, lubricating oil may help. The most resistant stand should be given to the stage directions reader, who generally has fewer adjustments to make. Music stands should be wiped clean with a damp cloth.

Directors spike music stands at an appropriate distance from each other and from the audience. Any tape that is easily seen can be used. Spiking the stands is useful even if rehearsals are not being held where the Reading will be performed. Upstage of the upstage leg of the tripod is the best place for the spike mark; if a music stand is moved, it can be repositioned by the actor. If rehearsals are held in a different room from where the Reading will be performed, the stands will need to be respiked.

Directors number the music stands stage left to stage right with masking tape on the upstage side of the desk so that the numbers are visible to the actors but not to the audience. The floor on the upstage side of each music stand can also be numbered.

When the producer, director, and stage manager do their work thoroughly in advance, the rehearsal period can be productive, not pressured.

The Actors

Actors arrive on time for rehearsal; they can arrive earlier if the venue is open. If dressing rooms are available, they store their belongings. Once settled, the actors inspect the venue and the playing area. If rehearsals are held in a different room than the Reading, the cast visits the performance venue to get a feel for it.

Most importantly, actors acquaint themselves with the music stands.

The significance of music stands for Play Readings cannot be overstated. While not required, for any Reading in which they are used, they are the actors' principle tool. Actors should manipulate all of the stands—raise them, lower them, adjust the angle of the desks. Just as in a full production where they would familiarize themselves with furniture and props, for a Reading, actors should be in complete control of the music stands.

Scripts are distributed to the cast. Some actors prefer to hold loose pages in their hands, even when binders are provided. This is not advisable. The audience should not have to wait during a Reading while actors reassemble spilled pages.

Certain actors may have printed out a copy of the script; they should check that their pagination matches that on the scripts that have been provided. This way, page numbers can be referred to easily throughout rehearsal. The actors highlight their lines in their scripts. Highlighters and pencils should be made available.

Pre-rehearsal Discussions

A playwright's presence in the room is important for a Reading rehearsal. Playwrights can quickly answer any questions. Every effort should be made for playwrights to be available for the full rehearsal period. If a writer cannot attend in person, Skype is the next best option, or they can listen to rehearsals by cell phone. If playwrights cannot participate for the entire rehearsal, they should offer introductory remarks.

Playwrights talk to the artistic team about the story they are trying to tell. They may choose to clarify the tone and style, say a few words about each of the characters and the relationships, and point out key moments.

Playwrights should let actors know what they would like to learn from the Reading. Are they unsure about certain scenes or beats? The playwright has discussed all of this with the director, but now actors are brought into the conversation. When writers are specific about what they hope to gain, directors and actors can assist them more purposefully. Playwrights should also clarify the pronunciation and definition of obscure terms. Actors should feel free to ask any questions. After the playwright addresses the cast, the director offers a few observations on the play and discusses the approach to rehearsal.

However, these conversations should be brief. There is no time for extended dialogue at a Play Reading rehearsal. If table work is necessary, then the play is not ready or not right for a Reading. Complex plays that require detailed examination are not well served by Readings: "The Coast of Utopia," for example. But playwrights who accept an offer do so with the conviction that a Reading will be of use.

For that to happen, rehearsal time needs to be monitored. Brief introductory remarks are helpful; an elaborate exegesis by the playwright or director and extensive questions from the actors are not. The short rehearsal demands that the creative team hit the ground running. Directors' and actors' spontaneous choices in rehearsal, even if they are misguided, can be helpful to playwrights.

> *It's best if the director doesn't talk too much before rehearsal for a reading begins. Five minutes at the most. Then open it up to the actors. Playwrights should also talk to the cast, to establish a personal connection. Readings are about the actors' tool-kits. Actors need to make strong choices. They have to make the script "pop" immediately. Over-rehearsing and over-thinking lead to*

bad choices. The most interesting choices come out instinctively at readings. Directors should give actors the confidence to tell the story, and provide an environment for creativity.

Jose Zayas, Director

Rehearsal Strategies

Directors may choose to start rehearsal by having the actors read through the entire script without stopping. This will often reveal which scenes will require attention and which will not. Then the artistic team can "stop-and-go," working through the script scene by scene, incorporating movement, discussing intention, and clarifying difficult beats. When the stop-and-go is complete, if time permits, the play can be run straight through.

Another approach is to read through the entire script without stopping, then review certain scenes or beats. Following this, instead of a stop-and-go, which takes more time, they could do a "cue-to-cue." The term is commonly use in technical rehearsals, but, as applied here, "cue" refers to entrances, exits, positions, and internal moves. After the read-through, the review, and the cue-to-cue, if time allows, the cast could run the play.

Or the director may choose to begin with a stop-and-go. Rather than reading through the play, the team works through the script scene by scene. Actors are given their entrances, music stand positions, internal moves, and exits. Discussing each scene before running it is not necessary, as many scenes will fall into place without conversation. After each scene, if need be, the director and playwright can offer notes, request adjustments, and answer questions from the actors and the reader.

Whatever the approach, actors must be discriminating in their questions, and playwrights and directors must be discerning in their notes. Carefully selecting which questions to ask and which notes to give is the hallmark of actors and directors who are skilled at Play Readings. Certain gifted artists cannot perform effectively within these parameters, while others thrive—or at least manage.

All good theatre is created by using time effectively; with Play Readings, the challenge is intensified. Unlike rehearsals for a full production where the play evolves over time and every comment is worth considering, for Readings, directors and actors should trust the script, and playwrights and directors should respect the actors' impulses. That is the challenge and the reward.

However, if an actor is misinterpreting the tone of a scene, or if the pacing or rhythm is off, a note is in order. And if actors are confused about the meaning or intention of any line or scene, questions are useful.

Often, in rehearsals for Readings, playwrights have more direct contact with actors than in production. During rehearsal, time is saved if playwrights answer actors' questions directly. But some directors prefer the full production approach. The playwright and director should agree on terms before rehearsals begin.

Protocol

I like to talk to actors in a reading rehearsal, but some directors say "Go through me first." Others say "The room is open." We both have to be sensitive to time. Actors make a choice and go with it.

If it's the wrong choice, someone has to stop them from going off the rail.

Caridad Svich, Playwright

I ask playwrights, "What would you like to hear? Would you like to hear this in a different way? Would you like more humor or irony?" Hopefully, I've helped playwrights. I say to them, "Tell me anything you want me to know about the character." If they want to hear it faster, I do it faster. If I'm on the wrong path, tell me. We're doing this for the playwright.

Lynn Cohen, Actor

In rehearsal for a reading, playwrights should talk directly to actors. When a playwright can step in and clarify something, don't be precious. When you hear a playwright talk about their play, you hear their voice.

Jose Zayas, Director

Whether the actors will be able to run through the entire play following any of these approaches depends on the amount of rehearsal time, the length of the play, and how well the creative team has used their time. An eight-hour rehearsal for a short play or a two-day rehearsal for a full-length play might allow for a run before the Reading, whereas a four-hour rehearsal for a full-length play may not. But it is essential that the artistic team works through the entire play before the performance.

Directors should go into rehearsal knowing what they want to achieve. If time remains, trouble spots can be revisited and reworked. The rehearsal should not feel rushed. Time should also be allocated to review challenging stage directions and incorporate any technical cues.

For many Readings of full-length plays, the first time the script is performed straight through is in front of the audience. It follows that some questions will be unanswered and some scenes or beats will be unclear. Playwrights can learn about their work from the extempore choices made by actors during the performance, where, by instinct, most actors will expand on their characterizations. That is part of what makes Play Readings exciting.

Impact of Audiences

Audiences impact the performance. I don't change anything—but it happens.

Lynn Cohen, Actor

With public readings, entertaining the audience is always the unstated goal.

Ian Morgan, Associate Artistic Director,
New Group

CHAPTER 8

MOVEMENT, GESTURES, AND ADAPTING STAGE DIRECTIONS IN REHEARSAL

As discussed, distributing Reading drafts to actors makes the best use of time. If the stage directions have been edited but the actors do not have Reading drafts, the edits for the entire play can be given to the actors at the start of rehearsal. Another approach is to provide actors with the edits for each scene before that scene is rehearsed. Actors should note all edits and revisions in the stage directions legibly in the scripts.

As the team works through the text, the playwright, director and actors explore each stage direction. Some will be eliminated or reinstated. Others may need to be revised or rewritten. If the director chose to wait until rehearsal, the creative team can edit collaboratively as they work through they play.

Together in rehearsal, the playwright, director, and actors decide exactly what the actors do when each stage direction is read.

The discussion of editing stage directions continues here with the scene from "Under the Mango Tree," using the placement and movement determined by the director as described in Part One. Below is a preliminary edit of the stage directions in the struck-through Reading draft, with explanations of the choices.

~~SCENE 18~~

~~TIME:~~ ONE WEEK LATER ~~LATE AFTERNOON~~

Speaking each scene number is optional. When a phrase referencing time or location follows, the scene number can generally be eliminated. Audiences do not need to tally up the number of scenes in a play. A phrase such as "One Week Later" tells the audience a new scene has begun, so in this case, "Scene 18" can be struck. Eliminating the scene number but keeping the word "Scene" is another option.

If a scene begins with no new information, eliminating the scene number might confuse audiences as to whether a new scene has started and thus, should be retained. But consistency is important; if one scene number is read, they all should be read, and if one is eliminated, they should all should be. If the audience hears "Scene 18" and "Scene 16" but did not hear about "Scene 17," they might wonder if a scene has been cut.

Given that the phrase "One Week Later" references time, the word "Time" is not necessary. And unless the time of day has a specific function in the scene, a phrase such as "Late Afternoon" can also be removed. "One Week Later" tells the audience when the scene takes place. Again, stage directions can only be edited effectively after a thorough examination of the script.

> *Gloria enters with a dress in her hand.*

This is necessary information. The director informs the actor playing Gloria that she will move on the stage direction *"Gloria enters with a dress in her hand."* When she hears the word *"Gloria"* spoken by the reader, the actor moves from retreat position to MS4.

An actor should move at the same time the stage direction is read. This allows the audience to focus on the actor while simultaneously hearing the content of the stage direction.

Gestures and Physicalization

Though Gloria moves to MS4 *"with a dress in her hand,"* the actor will not have a prop. To suggest the action, the actor playing Gloria could extend her arm as if she is carrying a dress (see Photograph 8.1). There is no need for the actor to execute this gesture; the stage direction will communicate the necessary information to the audience. If that is the director's choice, then throughout the Reading, no gestures should be enacted when stage directions are read.

However, if an actor does not gesture when an action is described in a spoken stage direction, the audience's focus will be diverted from that actor to the reader. With multiple stage directions, the audience will be required to continuously look back and forth from the actors to the reader, as if they are watching a tennis match. This can hurt the presentation.

If an actor gestures to suggest the action described in the stage direction when it is read, the focus remains on the actor. Just as in a production, an audience will look at someone moving rather than someone speaking. Simple gestures that suggest the action are useful in Play Readings. Many actors do this instinctively. At times, the director can assist the actor with determining the clearest gesture.

Gestures should always be visible to the audience—either above the music stands or between them.

One of the risks of gestures in Readings is that the actors resemble photographs from nineteenth-century acting texts such as "Siddon's Rhetorical Gestures." To avoid this, it is essential that gestures are natural and spontaneous. They should be informed by actor instinct and be specific to the character at that moment.

> GLORIA Hello I am here! It's Gloria . . . Hello
> 　　. . . Is ANYBODY home?!
> *Fela enters in her Sunday best.*

The actor playing Fela moves from her retreat position to MS6. The audience should know that she is in *"her Sunday best,"* as what the characters wear is important to the scene. The actor can suggest that she is dressed up when she moves into position, which will hold the audience's focus while the stage direction is read.

> FELA Hi Gloria.
> GLORIA I brought something for Lena. I hope she
> 　　likes it.

```
FELA Lena, there's someone here to see you. LENA!!
Lena enters patio.
```

Lena enters the patio, but she is not carrying or wearing anything of note. The actor moves from retreat position to MS7, which tells the audience she has entered. When actors move back and forth from retreat positions to music stands, stage directions such as *"enters"* or *"exits"* can be eliminated.

This may seem inconsistent, but it would be confusing if the audience did not know that Gloria is holding a dress, whereas when Lena moves to her assigned music stand, the audience will clearly see that she has entered. Eliminating as many stage directions as possible trumps consistency in cases such as these.

```
GLORIA Hi Lena.
LENA Hey.
GLORIA The dress is for you Lena—for the Fiesta of
        San Lorenzo.
LENA No way.
FELA You have to go the Fiesta, like a young lady.
LENA Ah man . . .
GLORIA I made it for you.
LENA/FELA What?
FELA Let me see.
Fela checks out dress.
```

Spoken stage directions for Readings are easier to understand when they are complete sentences, so the word *"the"* is added before *"dress."*

```
Fela checks out the dress.
```

As determined previously, Fela is near Gloria for the spoken stage direction *"Fela checks out the dress."* The director has decided that Fela takes the dress from Gloria (see Photograph 8.2).

An adjustment that might enhance the scene is for Fela and Gloria to angle their music stands toward each other and for Lena, who is resistant, to position her music stand straight out (see Photograph 8.3).

```
GLORIA It's my first "GLORIA"!
LENA You made it . . . my first dress, now I gotta
     wear it.
GLORIA You better.
```

Since Fela is holding the dress, she could make a simple gesture of draping it on the music stand after these lines or suspend the gesture. Actors in Readings should not sustain gestures for too long, which can look awkward. The gestures should be held long enough to communicate the action and then dropped. But given that Gloria takes the dress with her when she exits, the best choice is for Fela to hand it back to Gloria.

Photograph 8.1

Photograph 8.2

Photograph 8.3

Photograph 8.4

> *Felix enters—he brings flowers with him.*

Because of the flowers, this stage direction is necessary. As it is read, Felix moves from retreat position to MS5, gesturing to suggest that he is carrying flowers (see Photograph 8.4). Notice that the actor in retreat position is looking down at his script.

```
FELIX Hola . . .
FELA Hola Felix.
FELIX Thank you for inviting me. For you.
He gives her the flowers.
```

The audience knows from the spoken stage direction that Felix is holding flowers. A gesture can communicate that he gives the flowers to Fela, so the stage direction can be pruned. Later in the scene, Lena will take the flowers, so she can look in on the scene, revealing her interest (see Photograph 8.5).

If Gloria had not taken the dress back from Fela, both of Fela's hands would now be occupied. Not only would this look ungainly, but it would be difficult for the actor to turn the page without suspending one of the gestures. Directors should avoid requiring an actor to execute gestures with both hands. Again, the best choices are determined by studying the play. In this case, since Gloria will exit with the dress, Fela hands it back to her, and Gloria gestures draping it over MS4.

Actors need input into these decisions. They must be comfortable with any gesture asked of them. Also, the approach to these physical adjustments should be consistent throughout the Reading. Through the combination of spoken stage directions and gestures from the actors, the audience will visualize the dress and the flowers as these items move from character to character, all the while keeping their focus on the actors.

```
FELA Thank you. They're beautiful . . . I'm so
    sorry, I didn't mean to . . .
FELIX Don't say anything.
LENA I forgot something inside . . . um . . . let
    me bring the flowers inside . . .
```

Gloria gestures to release the flowers as Lena gestures to take them (see Photograph 8.6).

```
Lena exits back into the house.
```

The stage direction implies that Lena moves from her music stand to a retreat position. Since the move would tell the audience she has left the patio, the stage direction could be cut. But the character has more lines, so she should not be in retreat position yet, as discussed in Part One. Instead, she could take a step upstage of the music stand, suggesting that she is starting to exit. This is not an imperative move but a useful one. Either way, the stage direction can be eliminated.

```
LENA Gloria . . . come on . . .
GLORIA But . . .
LENA Would you come on already! Help me put on my
    dress!
```

Photograph 8.5

Photograph 8.6

```
GLORIA Stop bossing me around.
LENA You're the one that likes to boss people
    around.
They both exit into house.
```

Lena and Gloria exit to retreat positions. Lena is holding the flowers, and Gloria has the dress. They can sustain their gestures throughout the dialogue above and then suspend them. As previously determined, Fela is at MS6, and Felix is at MS5.

```
FELIX You look beautiful. Oh . . . I have
    something else for you.
Felix gives Fela a mango.
```

Fela's next line, *"A mango?"* tells the audience what Felix is giving her, so the stage direction is not needed. While Felix's generosity is admirable, where did this mango come from? Was he holding it along with the flowers when he entered? That would encumber the actor. He does not need to pantomime carrying a bag when he enters or reach into his pocket to retrieve the mango. A simple gesture of presenting a mango to Fela will suffice. (see Photograph 8.7).

```
FELA A mango?
FELIX Strangest thing . . . You know we couldn't
    chop down the tree? Some demolition specialist
    comes over—he hits the tree—the axe nicks it.
    He tells us the tree is alive. And sure enough
    the mangoes are fresh. Can you believe it?
FELA Fresh? . . . Life is . . . sometimes . . .
    very strange . . .
FELIX Telling me—couldn't cut down the tree so I
    finally had to pay off the Diaz family so that
    I could lay down the water pipe.
Fela smells mango as Belen enters.
```

Fela smells the mango (see Photograph 8.8) as Belen moves from her retreat position to MS1. Both of these actions will be clear to the audience without the stage directions.

```
BELEN Look at how handsome my grand . . . oye
    where are you? Junior get over here right
    now!!
Junior enters dressed in an elegant "white guaya-
    bera." It is a dress shirt commonly used in
    the Caribbean—with four pockets on the front
    of the shirt.
```

This stage direction can be simplified, but the audience should know that Junior is wearing a dress shirt.

```
Junior enters dressed in an elegant dress shirt.
```

Photograph 8.7

Photograph 8.8

The playwright might want the audience to know that the shirt is Caribbean.

```
Junior enters dressed in an elegant "white
   guayabera," ~~."  It is~~ a dress shirt commonly
   used in the Caribbean—with four pockets on
   the front of the shirt.
```

The audience does not need to know how many pockets are on the shirt.

```
Junior enters dressed in an elegant "white
   guayabera," ~~."  It is~~ a dress shirt commonly
   used in the Caribbean~~—with four pockets on~~
   ~~the front of the shirt~~.
```

A few additional tweaks can smooth out this stage direction. Since the word *"dress"* precedes *"shirt"* later in the sentence, cutting the first appearance of the word *"dressed"* helps the spoken line flow. Also, the word *"used"* is less precise than "worn," so with the playwright's permission, that can be changed.

```
Junior enters ~~dressed~~ in an elegant "white
   guayabera," ~~."  It is~~ a dress shirt commonly
   ~~used~~ worn in the Caribbean~~—with four pockets~~
   ~~on the front of the shirt~~.
```

When a stage direction is revised this substantially, the reader and the actor who has the next line (in this case, Junior) should write the entire revision in their scripts. Here is the final version:

```
Junior enters in an elegant "white guayabera," a
   dress shirt commonly worn in the Caribbean.
```

Junior enters and moves to MS2 while the stage direction is read, communicating the discomfort suggested by his first line in the scene. Apparently, the actor playing Lena, who should be looking at the script from retreat position, has left it at MS7 (see Photograph 8.9).

Actors should take their scripts whenever they relocate. When Lena reenters the scene, she will be positioned at a different music stand, so she would need to retrieve her script from MS7 first. Giving her the benefit of the doubt, Lena has only one more line in the play: Perhaps she memorized it.

```
JUNIOR I feel stupid.
BELEN Mira que handsome. I felt bad about punish-
   ing him so much so I bought him all these new
   clothes and a new basketball. He's teaching me
   to play. Verdad . . .
~~Belen gives him a nuggy.~~
```

Belen can perform this action with a gesture (although the playwright or director might need to explain to Belen exactly what a "nuggy" is) (see Photograph 8.10).

Photograph 8.9

Photograph 8.10

The stage directions reader may be tempted to look at the actors when they are doing something interesting. They should not. Apparently, the reader here could not resist (see Photograph 8.11).

```
JUNIOR Yeah, whatever.
FELIX Junior you look like a young man.
JUNIOR Thanks, I guess.
```

Next, Fela and Belen reconcile. As discussed earlier, the director decided that Felix and Junior will take a step upstage during this brief exchange.

```
BELEN Fela, I'm glad you called . . .
FELA Sh, sh—mija, you're like my sister, I'm sorry.
BELEN Esta bien.
FELA . . . Lena, Lena, Gloria, let's go . . .
Gloria enters.
```

Gloria moves from retreat position to MS4. There is no need for the stage direction. On her entrance, Junior and Felix can step forward to their previous music stand positions and return their focus to the scene.

```
GLORIA Attention everyone . . . Lena will be
    modeling an original "Gloria."
Lena enters with dress on, but she still wears
    her sneakers.
```

Since what Lena is wearing is important, the stage direction should be read as Lena moves from retreat position to MS4. This is a significant moment in the play, and all of the actors might look at Lena when she enters. Some actors would do this instinctively, but directors can make the request. Notice that Lena is in strong position center stage for the end of the play (see Photograph 8.12).

```
BELEN Oye, look how beautiful you two are. Lena,
    you're wearing a dress.
LENA Oh brother.
GLORIA We have to work on her footwear—pero the
    dress looks good huh?
JUNIOR Hi Lena.
```

The director decided that Junior would move from MS2 to MS3 on his line. That he is becoming interested in Lena as a woman will be conveyed to the audience by this move, which is of interest to the entire cast (see Photograph 8.13).

```
FELA We're all ready. Let's go!
```

This is the end of the play. The actors could stay in these positions for the curtain call, or they could move downstage between the music stands and take their bows in front of them, as discussed below.

Photograph 8.11

Photograph 8.12

Photograph 8.13

The movement and editing of stage directions outlined above are by no means the only options for this scene. Directors determine preliminary edits and map out the placement and movement of the actors for the entire play, preferably before rehearsal. Then, in collaboration with the actors, the stage directions and movement are adapted and refined, gestures are incorporated, and key moments are identified and articulated. This approach works well for most plays.

CHAPTER 9

EDITING AND MOVEMENT FOR CHALLENGING TEXT AND STAGE DIRECTIONS

Certain plays include requirements, either in the stage directions or the scripts themselves, which pose challenges in the limited rehearsal time offered for most Play Readings.

Common Challenges

- Long sequences without dialogue, where important information is revealed through action described in the stage directions
- Stage directions that depict physical action, either comic or dramatic
- Stage directions that involve intimacy
- Sound effects
- Singing in a nonmusical
- Foreign language dialogue
- Accents
- Unconventional stage directions.

If a play contains many sequences with challenging stage directions, directors should find simple, consistent solutions. If a play contains only a few such scenes and they are significant, it may be worthwhile to step beyond the established conventions of the proposed Play Reading model to convey the playwrights' intentions. Actors' input is important, and rehearsal time should be allocated.

Extended Stage Directions

Many plays contain an extended sequence where no dialogue is spoken and multiple actions occur. Such scenes may inform the content or tone of the play. Below is an example of such a scene from "Death by Design" as it appears in the published script. It includes a lengthy stage direction describing a comic dance.

> VICTORIA I shall demonstrate. *(to EDWARD)* You, de
>   Sade—beat the table, thus. *(she demonstrates,*
>   *beating the table with her hand)* Beating is

within your area of expertise. *(to ERIC)* And
you, tousled youth—shake the ice bucket. I
will create an improvised work, using the
latest modern dance techniques. It shall be
called—"Wall."

EDWARD Walter, would you care to participate?

WALTER I prefer to sit on the sidelines and watch.

VICTORIA *(to WALTER, firmly)* Stand, man.

WALTER Now, just a minute.

VICTORIA I said stand!

VICTORIA reveals her unshaven armpit. WALTER,
frightened, jumps up and obeys. VICTORIA indi-
cates a place for him to stand.

VICTORIA You represent Wall.

SOREL You have the title role, Walter. That's very
good!

WALTER Do you mean that I'm—a partition?

VICTORIA You are a barrier—an obstruction.

SOREL Victoria, what part am I to play?

VICTORIA *(improvising)* You shall be Tree, casting
a shadow over Wall.

SOREL *(intrigued)* What sort of Tree? A Royal
Empress, perhaps?

EDWARD A Dogwood, with age rings.

VICTORIA Tree will respond intuitively to the inner
meaning of the piece through the movement of
her branches.

SOREL I embrace the challenge!

VICTORIA Art is nigh! Let us commence!

EDWARD bangs the table and ERIC shakes the ice
bucket, providing a rhythmic accompaniment to
VICTORIA's dance. SOREL stands and assumes
the role of Tree, with her arms spread like
limbs. JACK and BRIDGIT watch, perplexed.
VICTORIA moves about the room slowly, in
sweeping, Martha Graham-like moves, stop-
ping with exaggerated poses every now and
then near WALTER, "struggling" to suggest
through dance that she cannot get around him.
She is intensely serious, and occasionally
rearranges her scarf with her arms, creat-
ing web-like shapes. WALTER remains stiff and
wall-like. He is annoyed, but doesn't want
to disappoint SOREL. EDWARD is amused by WAL-
TER's discomfort. SOREL, as Tree, adjusts
her limbs as she tries to interpret VICTO-
RIA's intentions. BRIDGIT and JACK remain

```
perplexed. In one of her moves, VICTORIA
nearly swipes BRIDGIT's head with her arm,
but she ducks just in time. After a few min-
utes, during which WALTER becomes increas-
ingly uncomfortable, VICTORIA approaches
WALTER and in one quick move, completely
smothers his head in her scarf.
```

First, the director and playwright need to decide how important this scene is for the Reading.

If it is one of many such scenes, it should be pared down considerably. If the scene is distinct, and useful for either dramatic or comic purposes, it should be included but simplified. Various options can be considered.

The easiest solution would be for the stage directions reader to deliver this entire passage and attempt to bring the scene to life vocally. This would require lively inflection. However, the audience would focus on the person reading stage directions for a long while, leaving the actors stranded.

The director could decide there should be movement during this scene. Victoria might move away from her music stand. As the comedy described is inherently physical, some movement seems appropriate. In his or her diagram in the script, the director can outline what the actors might do while each stage direction is read and generate a preliminary edit.

To fully stage this sequence would require considerable time. But with minimal rehearsal, the director and cast can conjure up something that conveys the tone and style of the scene, which merely reading the stage directions would not. As always, but even more so in scenes such as this, the final decisions will be based on what the director and actors discover in rehearsal.

```
VICTORIA I shall demonstrate. (to EDWARD) You, de
    Sade—beat the table, thus. (she demonstrates,
    beating beats the table with her hand)
```

The actor playing Victoria might bang the music stand or stomp her foot as the stage direction is read. Notice that the word *"beating"* has been changed to *"beats"* because *"she demonstrates"* has been cut. Also, note that *"to EDWARD"* and *"to ERIC"* (below) are cut. Victoria can direct her focus to these characters when she addresses them.

A stage direction such as *"to Edward"* should rarely be spoken in a Reading. If this type of edit might result in confusion as to whom a character is addressing, with the playwright's permission, the character's name can be added to the line for the Reading, as in, "Edward. Yes, you, de Sade . . ."

```
VICTORIA Beating is within your area of
    expertise. (to ERIC) And you, tousled youth—
    shake the ice bucket. I will create an
    improvised work, using the latest modern
    dance techniques. It shall be called—"Wall."
EDWARD Walter, would you care to participate?
```

```
WALTER I prefer to sit on the sidelines and watch.
VICTORIA (to WALTER, firmly) Stand, man.
WALTER Now, just a minute.
VICTORIA I said stand!
VICTORIA reveals her unshaven armpit.
```

Earlier in the play, the audience learned that Victoria shaves only one of her armpits, so this stage direction should also be shaved. Victoria can lift her arm.

```
WALTER, frightened, jumps up and obeys. VICTORIA
     indicates a place for him to stand.
VICTORIA You represent Wall.
SOREL You have the title role, Walter. That's very
     good.
WALTER Do you mean that I'm a partition?
VICTORIA You are a barrier—an obstruction.
SOREL Victoria, what part am I to play?
VICTORIA (improvising) You shall be Tree, casting
     a shadow over Wall.
SOREL (intrigued) What sort of Tree? A Royal
     Empress, perhaps?
EDWARD A Dogwood, with age rings.
VICTORIA Tree will respond intuitively to the inner
     meaning of the piece through the movement of
     her branches.
SOREL I embrace the challenge!
VICTORIA Art is nigh! Let us commence!
EDWARD bangs the table and ERIC shakes the ice
     bucket, providing a rhythmic accompaniment to
     VICTORIA's dance. SOREL stands and assumes
     the role of Tree, with her arms spread like
     limbs.
```

Edward can bang on his music stand or stomp his foot as Victoria did previously, or he can make a gesture that suggests banging. Eric can position his hands as if he is shaking an ice bucket, and Sorel can spread her arms and pose as a tree. All this would happen as the stage direction is read (see Photograph 9.1).

```
JACK and BRIDGIT watch, perplexed.
```

Adverbs that suggest how an actor reacts, such as *"perplexed," "annoyed,"* and *"amused"* are often unnecessary. But if this stage direction is cut, the focus would likely shift to Victoria, who is dancing. Some phrases that seem likely candidates for editing might be amusing when spoken by the reader and accompanied by facial expressions and physical adjustments from the actors (see Photograph 9.2).

Photograph 9.1

```
VICTORIA moves about the room ~~slowly, in~~
     ~~sweeping, Martha Graham-like moves,~~ stopping
     with exaggerated poses every now and then
     near WALTER, "struggling" to suggest ~~through~~
     ~~dance~~ that she cannot get around him.
```

The actor playing Victoria can leave her music stand and weave around the other actors, who remain positioned. Her moves should not be extravagant as she may bump into someone, but she can display the comic intention of the dance. This could continue for a while if the actor is skilled at the dance, or it could be a short sequence. Again, rehearsal will reveal the best choice. If extended, the stage direction could be broken up.

```
VICTORIA moves about the room ~~slowly, in~~
     ~~sweeping, Martha Graham-like moves.~~
```

Victoria dances around the other characters in the manner described (see Photograph 9.3). Regarding the edit, the audience does not need to hear a reference to the choreographer who inspired Victoria's dance. The director can find video clips of Martha Graham and send research links to the actor before rehearsal.

The actor and director should determine the specific moment when the reader resumes speaking.

```
~~stopping~~ She stops with an exaggerated pose
     ~~every now and then~~ near WALTER, "struggling"
     to suggest ~~through dance~~ that she cannot
     get around him. ~~WALTER remains stiff and~~
     ~~wall-like.~~
```

The stage direction is edited and revised so that the pose happens once. Walter has been stiff and wall-like throughout the dance, so that reference can be shelved.

```
~~She is intensely serious, and occasionally~~
     ~~rearranges her scarf with her arms, creating~~
     ~~web-like shapes.~~
```

Victoria can express intense seriousness. If she is using a scarf, it might be worth trying a few *"web-like shapes,"* but either way, the entire sentence can be struck.

```
He is annoyed, but doesn't want to disappoint
     SOREL.
```

Reading the stage direction would shift the audience's focus from Victoria to Walter and Sorel. It might be comical for Walter to exaggerate his stiffness when the stage direction *"He is annoyed"* is read. As for *"but doesn't want to disappoint SOREL,"* Walter could smile meekly at Sorel, which would leave the entire stage direction intact (see Photograph 9.4).

```
~~EDWARD is amused by WALTER's discomfort.~~
```

Photograph 9.2

Photograph 9.3

Photograph 9.4

Photograph 9.5

As for Edward's reaction, the choice of whether to include this stage direction is similar to those which determined the other characters' reactions. Consistency would suggest that if *"JACK and BRIDGIT watch, perplexed"* and *"He (WALTER) is annoyed"* are read, then *"EDWARD is amused by WALTER's discomfort"* should also be read. But these decisions are also informed by the actors' ability to execute these attitudes and the director's assessment of their comic impact. The best choice may be to eliminate some stage directions that reference reactions and keep others.

Meanwhile, is Edward still banging the table and is Eric still shaking the ice bucket? If Edward's *"banging"* and Eric's *"shaking"* are not distracting, the actors can continue these moves throughout the scene. If the continuous *"banging"* and *"shaking"* make too much noise, look clumsy, or pull focus, the actors can suspend these moves soon after they are identified.

> SOREL, ~~as Tree,~~ adjusts her limbs as she tries to
> interpret VICTORIA's intentions.

It might be fun to watch Sorel readjust her limbs as the stage direction is read. But if the sequence feels long, it could easily be cut as she has likely been posing as Tree throughout, a move easier to sustain than *"banging"* or *"shaking."*

> ~~BRIDGIT and JACK remain perplexed.~~

Given that these characters have previously been described as *"perplexed,"* this stage direction is repetitive. But if it is read, the actors' perplexed look should be exaggerated.

> ~~In one of her moves, VICTORIA nearly swipes~~
> ~~BRIDGIT's head with her arm, but she ducks~~
> ~~just in time.~~

This swipe and duck would be clear without the stage direction (see Photograph 9.5). Note that Victoria is the only actor who moved from her music stand. In production, the other actors would likely change positions, but for a Reading, one actor navigating through a forest of music stands is sufficient.

> ~~After a few minutes, during which WALTER becomes~~
> ~~increasingly uncomfortable,~~ VICTORIA
> approaches WALTER and in one quick move,
> completely smothers his head in her scarf.

The stage direction describing the duration of time and Walter's increasing discomfort are expendable. The audience does not need to know the former, and the actor can convey the latter. But the last beat of the dance is important to bring the sequence to a satisfying conclusion.

Victoria can approach Walter and execute the action in the stage direction as it is read. If the director provided a scarf, or asked the actor playing Victoria to bring one to rehearsal, this entire episode could be performed using the scarf, as in the photographs, including the final beat (see Photograph 9.6).

This is an example of how a single prop can have impact, particularly given that later in the play, Victoria attempts to strangle Walter with the scarf. The director and the actor playing Victoria could rehearse the scene using a scarf to see if it can be done easily and efficiently. If not, the scarf could be cut (see Photograph 9.7).

Photograph 9.6

Photograph 9.7

With or without the scarf, the dance needs to be worked through carefully. In rehearsal, the director and the actors finalize which stage directions are read and which are not and exactly what moves and reactions are made throughout. The sequence requires more movement than is typical for a standard Reading. Rehearsal time should be allotted to run it more than once so that the actors and the reader have the correct edits in their scripts, the moves are executed safely, and Victoria's improvised dance has a satisfying finale.

Intimacy, Singing, and Sharing Music Stands

Just as in a full production, in a Reading, plays that involve physical intimacy need to be handled with care. Actors have different levels of comfort with intimate scenes, and Readings do not allow them time to become acquainted as they would in a full rehearsal. Even something as simple as a kiss can be tricky. Actors should not be required to do anything that makes them uneasy.

Below is an intimate scene from "Salt in a Wound," with suggestions as to how the action described in the stage directions might be edited and communicated for a Play Reading. (See Appendix G.)

```
JITTER Don't you understand, Julia? I want to
     take you places. Show you off like a man's
     s'posed to with the woman he love. I want to
     be able to walk down the street with you on
     my arm. Show the world that you my woman.
     Let everybody know that I'm your man. I
     don't want to hide it like it's something I'm
     shamed of. I want to shout it at the top of
     my lungs, JULIA WILLIAMS MY WOMAN, AND I'M
     PROUD TO BE HER MAN!
Julia looks around nervously.
JITTER (louder) JULIA WILLIAMS MY WOMAN, AND I'M
     PROUD TO BE HER MAN!
JULIA Hush! Somebody'll hear you.
JITTER Let 'em hear. JULIA WILLIAMS MY WO—
JULIA Jitter, please! Just give me a little more
     time. Please? I'll talk to Ma. I promise. I
     just need to do it when the time is right.
JITTER To hear you tell it, won't never be a right
     time for your mama.
Julia gives him a coquettish, pleading look.
JITTER Aw, woman, look at me like that, you ask for
     the world, I'd give it to ya.
(picks her up, swings her around)
```

For consistency, the stage direction should be rewritten as a full sentence:

```
Jitter picks her up and swings her around.
```

A few options present themselves. The stage direction can be read without any physical adjustment from the actors. They could simply make eye contact when it is read (see Photograph 9.8).

Photograph 9.8

Photograph 9.9

Another option is for Julia to spin around when the stage direction is spoken. The focus stays on the actors, and the intention is conveyed. The actor playing Julia must be comfortable with this move; if not, something simpler will suffice (see Photograph 9.9).

Either of these approaches is valid, and both let the actors look up from their scripts.

> JITTER But don't take too long, baby, cuz I can't
> wait much longer. ~~(sings)~~

When a Reading of a straight play requires a character to sing, the director or playwright should research the song and send a link or MP3 to the actor before rehearsal. Most straight plays that include songs do not require trained singers, so actors cast in Readings of these plays can usually meet the singing requirements. The song might also be edited, and just a line or two sung.

If locating the specific song is not possible, in a case such as this, singing almost any melody that suggests the tone of the scene will do. If that is difficult for the actor, he can speak the lines as if he were reciting a poem.

> JITTER Loveliest gal I ever did see.
> *(kisses her on the lips)*

A full sentence is best:

> *He kisses her on the lips.*

In rehearsal, some actors will instinctively kiss when a stage direction describes that action. But the two actors may feel differently about kissing, putting one of them in an uncomfortable position. Running scenes without previous discussion is often effective, but scenes that involve intimacy are exceptions. Before rehearsing the scene, the director and the actors should agree upon how these moments will be handled.

The scene becomes more sexual as it proceeds, so even if the actors want to kiss at this moment, the director should discourage it. A better option is for Jitter to move to Julia's music stand when the stage direction "*He kisses her on the lips*" is read. Two actors sharing a music stand can suggest intimacy in a Play Reading. Julia and Jitter could share the stand for the remainder of the scene.

When actors share a music stand, they should also share a script (see Photograph 9.10). Jitter's lines should be highlighted in Julia's script in a different color than her lines.

> JITTER Picked from the heavens you must be,
> *The kiss becomes passionate.*

The actors should not kiss passionately, an action which is outside the parameters of a Reading. They can look at each other longingly when this stage direction is read. A stronger choice might be for the actors to place their faces cheek to cheek (see Photograph 9.11).

Photograph 9.10

Photograph 9.11

This is more than a gesture—it is physical contact, and the actors should agree to this when discussing the scene with the director before rehearsing it.

    JITTER Sweeter than honey stole from a bee.
    Passion brings them slowly to the floor, him on
        top of her.

Unless the playwright feels that *"him on top of her"* is crucial, this stage direction should be eliminated. In a full production, the moment would likely be powerful. In a Reading, hearing it aloud is more information than the audience needs.

    Passion brings them slowly to the floor, ~~him on~~
        ~~top of her.~~

During this stage direction, Jitter might put his arm behind Julia's back, moving her closer to him, implying the described action and increasing intimacy (see Photograph 9.12)

    He breaks the embrace & looks into her eyes.

The stage direction can be cut if Jitter takes his arm from Julia's waist but stays at her music stand.

    ~~He breaks the embrace & looks into her eyes.~~
    JITTER Marry me woman—I'm begging ya, please.
    Julia looks at Jitter first in shock, then dis-
        belief, almost questioning if she heard him
        correctly.

Julia can communicate all of the actions described in the stage direction below.

    ~~Julia looks at Jitter first in shock, then~~
        ~~disbelief, almost questioning if she heard~~
        ~~him correctly.~~
    He smiles, strokes her hair and nods, then kisses
        her gently on the lips again. She returns the
        kiss. The lights fade as their passion rises.

If Jitter *"smiles, strokes her hair and nods,"* the first phrase in the stage direction can be cut. As for the remainder, this is the final beat of the scene and a key moment in the play. A light kiss on the lips is appropriate, but the actors should not be required or even encouraged to do this. The decision is made collaboratively. If either of the actors is disinclined, with their approval, Jitter could kiss Julia on the cheek (see Photograph 9.13).

As for *"She returns the kiss,"* Julia could embrace him (see Photograph 9.14).

Whatever actions or gestures the actors execute during this sequence, the goal is to keep the focus entirely on Jitter and Julia. Particularly at the end of the scene, any spoken stage directions might seem intrusive, almost voyeuristic. Such moments in Play Readings are well served by eliminating stage directions entirely.

Photograph 9.12

Photograph 9.13

Photograph 9.14

Whatever physical vocabulary the director and actors create to reveal the writer's intentions, these final beats are best enacted in silence, as they would be in production.

```
He smiles, strokes her hair and nods, then kisses
    her gently on the lips again. She returns the
    kiss.
The lights fade as their passion rises.
```

Jitter could remain at Julia's music stand through "*The lights fade as their passion rises*" and then move to retreat position as the next stage direction is read.

```
In the dark we hear Ma calling for Julia. When
    lights rise we find Julia lying in the same
    spot we just saw her in with Jitter, only now
    it is a few weeks later and she is alone in
    her bedroom.
```

Ma calls out for Julia after "*The lights fade as their passion rises,*" so the stage direction is unnecessary.

```
In the dark we hear Ma calling for Julia.
```

A slight edit allows the remainder of the stage direction to read more smoothly.

```
When lights rise we find Julia lying in the same
    spot. we just saw her in with Jitter, only
    now It is a few weeks later and she is alone
    in her bedroom.
```

```
MA Julia! What the devil are you doing? It's half
    past nine.
JULIA I was sleepin'.
MA You been sleepin' an awful lot lately.
JULIA I'm tired.
MA Who ain't.
JULIA But Ma, it's Saturday.
MA Life don't take pause on Saturday and chores
    don't stop just cuz you tired. What's gotten
    into you, girl?
JULIA (tentatively) Ma . . . you miss Pa?
MA What kinda fool question is that?
```

The approach outlined above is not the only way this sequence could be presented in a Reading of "Salt in a Wound." With all scenes involving intimacy or sexual content, directors must be tactful. They should discuss the scene with the actors before rehearsing it, and, collaboratively, the director and actors decide which moves and physical adjustments are most suitable. If the actors have different ideas, the director must defer to the actor who prefers the least intimacy.

The audience for a Reading will not expect the actions described in these stage directions to be fully executed; they would likely be startled if they were.

Many actors are more comfortable suggesting romantic interest than sexual attraction in a Reading, as the photographs from "Salt in a Wound" reveal. Romance is a suitable substitute for lust in a Play Reading. The spoken stage directions provide all the information the audience needs.

While the approach to any scene should be compatible with that for the entire Reading, for a key moment such as this, stepping outside the conventions of the model by incorporating physical contact is worth exploring.

However, rehearsing such scenes is time consuming. Only key scenes in the play should receive this type of detailed treatment. If an entire play consists of scenes that involve extended stage directions such as that in "Death by Design," intimacy such as the scene from "Salt in a Wound," or violence as in the scene from "Mama's Boy" below, directors should default to consistent choices that take the least time to rehearse.

Violence, Accents, Foreign Languages, and Sound Effects

The scene from "Mama's Boy" poses a variety of challenges in a Play Reading, including physical violence, the use of a foreign language, and, once again, intimacy and singing in a nonmusical. (See Appendix G.) Here is the preliminary edit of the stage directions:

> MARINA hands MARGUERITE one of the rolls of paper
> towels. ~~MARGUERITE exits, and~~ MARINA returns
> June to the dresser drawer.

Marina makes a gesture of handing a roll of paper towels to Marguerite, who returns to her retreat position. Marina then gestures putting the baby into a dresser drawer, which should be near her music stand.

> LEE reemerges ~~from the bathroom~~. His shirt, socks
> and shoes are off, and his hair is wet.

Lee moves from retreat position to his music stand. The audience heard him say earlier he was going to "wash up," so the phrase *"from the bathroom"* can be flushed. That he is partially undressed relates to the sexual nature of the scene, so this information should be retained.

> MARINA She is very alone woman, Lee.
> LEE I told you don't tell her where we lived.
> MARINA I no tell.
> LEE I said if she came not to let her in.
> MARINA Is no right.

Marina is from Russia. Her speech patterns reveal that English is not her first language. Casting an actor who has experience with a Russian accent would be ideal. If that is not possible, directors or playwrights can provide research materials. This would be effective in a play like "Mama's Boy," where Marina is the only character who speaks with this accent. If everyone in the play spoke with a Russian accent, achieving consistency would be difficult.

If a play requires all or most of the actors to speak with same accent, casting actors who have experience with that accent is the best choice. In these cases, the accent should not be as full as it would be for a full production. Every word in a Play Reading must be clearly understood, and thick accents, even when well executed, can impede intelligibility. In a full production, accents are refined in rehearsal, often with a dialect coach. But for a Play Reading, a suggestion of an accent is best.

When even a slight accent proves too challenging, they can be eliminated for a Reading. Most playwrights write dialogue for characters who speak with accents using word choice and sentence structure that reveal that character's native tongue. Modifying or doing away with accents will not harm a Play Reading.

```
LEE You don't know how she is. She won't stop
      till she squeezes everything out of me.
MARINA You have big secret?
LEE Are you gonna start with me now too?
MARINA Be nice, eh?
LEE With both of you henpecking me?
MARINA Shame on you! Shame!
LEE Do what I say.
MARINA I do what I want!
LEE slaps MARINA across the face. She lunges for
      him and punches him ferociously. He pulls
      away and collapses on the sofa. June cries.
      MARINA picks her up and rocks her. After a
      while:
```

Lee's rage escalates. He strikes his wife for the first time, a crucial moment in the play that should be carefully articulated in the Reading.

When doing a reading with violence, I subscribe to the "less is more" theory. Nothing should be fully staged so as to look "real." Simple acts (a slap, a push, a single punch) can be indicated with the actors staying well away from each other, although it is fine to add a knap (the sound of the hit). More complicated sequences should be read as stage directions. Anything too realistic takes us out of the reading and disrupts the flow.

Ted deChatelet, Fight Choreographer;
Actor; Director; Professor, Western Oregon University

The simplest choice is for Lee to adjust the angle of his music stand and glare at Marina when the stage direction is read (see Photograph 9.15). Notice that Marina is wearing a scarf during this scene. Unlike the scarf in "Death by Design," this was not a deliberate choice, but one borne of necessity. The actor playing Marina has braids and purple hair, so a decision was made to cover her hair with a character-appropriate scarf.

Another choice is when the stage direction is spoken, Lee could raise his hand to strike Marina, stopping before his hand reaches her face. When his hand

Photograph 9.15

Photograph 9.16

freezes, Marina could turn her face to the side as if she has been struck (see Photograph 9.17).

Lee could accompany this gesture by simply clapping his hand once, or with a knap by hitting the upstage side of his leg with his other hand. This would be similar to how the moment might be staged in a full production, with one crucial difference: The actors are at a safe distance from each other. Another approach is for Marina to make a knap by clapping her hands as she raises them to her face in a defensive gesture. Lee could also make the slapping gesture from a safe distance, while Marina turns her head as if she has been hit, vocalizing a response.

These are all effective choices for suggesting violence in a Play Reading and are relatively easy to rehearse. Whatever the decision, the first sentence in the stage direction "*LEE slaps MARINA across the face,*" should be read in its entirety so the audience fully understands the action. In most scenes involving violence, the stage direction description should be maintained because the violence will not be enacted. In the case of an extended fight, some of the stage directions can be cut, keeping just enough to convey the intention.

She lunges for him and punches him ferociously.

The simplest choice is for Marina to stare malevolently at Lee as the stage direction is read. She could also cross to his music stand confrontationally. That she fights back after she has been struck is significant, which this move would reveal. Marina might also execute a series of moves that suggest she is "*punching him ferociously.*" If she does, she should keep her distance. If she approaches him, she could execute the move in slow motion, or it could be a pose rather than continuous movement. Posing or freezing a violent gesture is safer in a Reading than following through with the action (see Photograph 9.16).

In a full production of a play with scenes that involve violence, the goal is to make the fight convincing and keep the actors are safe. A director and a fight choreographer, with input from the actors and sufficient rehearsal time, can achieve that. In a Reading, the safest and most effective way to execute fight choreography is to keep the actors apart and on their feet, even when a stage direction states specifically that a character falls or is thrown to the ground. Within these parameters, viable options exist.

In this scene from "Mama's Boy," whatever choices are made, the stage direction "*She lunges for him and punches him ferociously*" is read.

~~He pulls away and collapses on the sofa.~~

That Lee pulls away is important and could be conveyed simply if he moves to another music stand, leaving an unattended stand between himself and Marina. Where he collapses is not essential, so the entire stage direction could be cut. Here again, the moment is more powerful in silence.

June cries.

In a production, the audience would hear a sound cue of a baby crying. A director for a Reading should avoid sound cues. Even when technical support is available, sound effects are not necessary. There are exceptions; on occasion, as

Photograph 9.17

with a significant prop or costume piece, an important sound can be incorporated into a Reading.

Stage directions that reference a sound cue can be read, as in *"June cries," "An alarm sounds,"* or *"There is an explosion from upstairs."* For certain cues, the stage directions reader can make the described sound instead of reading the stage direction. For example, rather than saying *"A phone rings,"* the reader could make the sound of a phone ringing, and suggest the quality of the sound at that moment in the play. In a dramatic scene, for example, he or she might say "Ring! Ring!" with urgency. In a comedy, it may be appropriate for the stage directions reader to cry like a baby, but in a drama such as "Mama's Boy," it would be rather silly. So it is best if *"June cries"* is read as is.

At a crucial moment such as this, the director and actors need to decide exactly how much time should pass before the reader breaks the silence. A spoken stage direction should not prematurely intrude on a dramatic moment. Lee and Marina are recovering from a brutal attack on each other. June could cry immediately, but a few beats of silence may be potent. Once a decision is reached in rehearsal, the reader can be given a visual cue (such as "when Lee returns to his music stand") or an amount of time (as in "after ten seconds") to know when to resume.

> ~~MARINA lifts her from the dresser drawer and~~
> ~~rocks her. After a while:~~

This action is easily communicated through gesture, so the stage direction can be cut (see Photograph 9.18). Stage directions that denote a short passage of time, such as *"After a while," "A moments later," "Pause,"* or *"After a few beats,"* should generally be struck from a Reading. Playwrights include this type of stage direction when silence between the characters has weight. After Lee and Marina's confrontation, the characters need *"a while"* to recover. If the reader interrupts the silence by speaking the stage direction, the moment is compromised. The actors, with suggestions from the director, can fill these silent beats purposefully. In this case, Marina is rocking the baby. Perhaps Lee looks at Marina, and she catches his eye and looks away. The director and actors determine when the reader should resume.

While meaningful pauses in a Reading can be valuable, frequent pauses, unless they are essential for the tone or content of the play, can be damaging. Some playwrights use beats and pauses extensively in their stage directions. This is the writer's prerogative, and in rehearsal for a full production, each of these would be explored. For a Reading, eliminating or tightening most pauses is preferable. Actors can keep the silent beats physically alive.

> LEE I'm sorry, Mama.
> MARINA You are monster.
> LEE Forgive me?
> MARINA No.
> LEE Please.
> MARINA Why you hit? You never hit before.
> LEE I hate it here. It's worse than Russia.
> MARINA Russia no good. America no good. You only
>   happy on the moon, eh?

Photograph 9.18

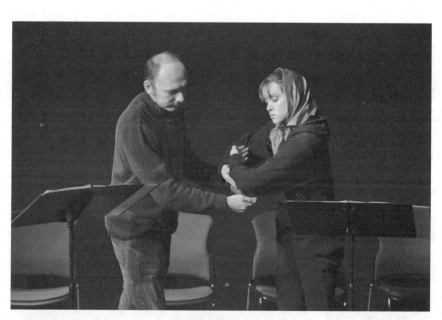

Photograph 9.19

LEE I want to move to Cuba.
MARINA ~~(incredulous)~~ Now is Cuba? Just like that—
    snap, crackle, pop?
LEE I'm gonna fight for Castro.
MARINA How you get to Cuba? We have no money for
    food.
LEE I'll hijack a plane.
MARINA ~~(a beat, then)~~ This is joke, right?

Marina needs a moment to figure out if Lee is serious. This is another example of a "passage of time" stage direction that should be cut. Marina can easily convey her confusion over his remark.

LEE Come with me, Mama.
MARINA If I say no?
LEE I'll go by myself.
MARINA Find new job, Alik. The Russians, they help.
    Robert help.
LEE I don't want their help.
MARINA Big shot.
LEE Marina, I have nothing—what have I got to lose?
MARINA Me and Junie—this is nothing?
LEE I want to come home from work with clean hands
    and hold my little girl-
MARINA We have sink and soup.
LEE Soap.
MARINA You wash hands with soap, eh?
LEE ~~(tenderly)~~ Give her to me.
~~MARINA hesitates, then hands June to LEE. June~~
    ~~stops crying. MARINA softens.~~

Marina can hesitate before handing June to Lee. Then the actors physically convey that she hands the baby to him (see Photograph 9.19).

The next part of the stage direction, *"June stops crying,"* suggests that the baby has been crying throughout the scene. Not hearing June cry, the audience likely forgot about it, so *"June stops crying,"* which would remind them of what they did not hear, can be eliminated. Alternatively, *"June stops crying"* could be spoken. That the baby stops crying when her father holds her motivates the next stage direction, *"Marina softens."* Either choice will work for *"June stops crying,"* but *"Marina softens"* should be conveyed by the actor.

June stops crying. ~~MARINA softens.~~
MARINA What if Junie no open door for you when she
    is big girl?
LEE Junie loves me, right Unka?
MARINA She sleep now.
She takes June and puts her back in the dresser
    drawer.

This information is useful, as Marina needs to be unencumbered for the remainder of the scene. The actor can suggest that she takes June from Lee and returns her to the dresser drawer, which, as previously noted, is nearby.

```
LEE Come sit with me, Mama.
MARINA sits next to him. He tries to kiss her and
    she brushes him away.
```

Lee moved away from Marina earlier, on "*He pulls away and collapses on the sofa,*" so if she relocates to the unattended music stand next to him, this part of the stage direction is not needed. "*He tries to kiss her and she brushes him away*" can be easily communicated.

```
MARINA sits next to him. He tries to kiss her and
    she brushes him away.
Softly, LEE sings some of an aria from "The Queen
    of Spades," as he gets on his knees, caress-
    ing her feet.
LEE (singing, in Russian)
```

Ja lublu tebja, Ja lublu tebja neizmerimo.
Ja ne mogu sebe predstavit' svoej zhizni bez tebja.

```
(singing, in English)
```

I am ready right now to perform a heroic deed
Of unprecedented prowess for your sake
I am ready to conceal my feelings to please you
I am ready to do anything for your sake
Not only to be a husband, but a servant.

The stage direction before the song poses multiple challenges: the character sings an aria from an opera in Russian as he caresses his wife's feet. It can be useful to divide up stage directions such as these and solve each issue separately.

For a Reading, an actor can be asked to learn to speak a few lines written in a foreign language. If the actor agrees, the director or playwright should provide a research link to audio of the spoken text before rehearsal. Such a request should only be made with a limited amount of dialogue. Actors should not be asked to learn extensive text in a language not their own. If an actor agrees, they should come to rehearsal having studied the correct pronunciation of the lines.

The easiest solution in a Play Reading involving a foreign language is for the reader to identify the character and the language before the sequence that includes these lines, for example, "Fernando's lines are spoken in Spanish." Then the actor playing Fernando would read his lines in English.

A playwright may feel strongly that the audience should hear the lines as they appear in the script to get a feel for the language. If the actor is unable to learn the lines, someone who speaks the language can be added to the cast. This actor could say each line as written, then the actor playing the role could speak the lines translated into English. The additional actor could be seated opposite the person reading stage directions. This approach would only work for a short scene.

Another option is for the stage directions reader to speak the lines, which would inform that casting choice. Playwrights, directors, and actors must work to find practical solutions, as more and more plays are bilingual or multilingual.

As for the singing, the audience should know that Lee is familiar with this opera—in fact, he has committed the aria to memory. Ideally, the playwright or director could provide the actor with links to the music and the Russian pronunciation of the first two lines, and the actor playing Lee could sing the aria in Russian. But this is a lot to ask of an actor for a Reading. Singing even part of an aria is considerably more demanding than singing a popular song, although here, as in "Salt in a Wound," a full production of the play would not require a trained singer. While the request is appropriate, the actor playing Lee may be unable to sing the aria in either language. Instead, he can speak the lyrics.

If the actor can deliver the lines in Russian, the reader would say, "*Softly, LEE sings some of an aria from "The Queen of Spades."* In this case, the Russian lyrics would not need to be translated. If the actor cannot speak the lines in Russian, the stage direction could be revised to read, "*Softly, in Russian, LEE sings some of an aria from "The Queen of Spades,"* and Lee would read the translated lyrics.

LEE *(singing, in Russian)*

Ja lublu tebja, Ja lublu tebja neizmerimo.
[I love you, I love you immeasurably]
Ja ne mogu sebe predstavit' svoej zhizni bez tebja.
[I cannot imagine my life without you]

At this point, the reader would say, "*Lee continues singing, now in English.*"

I am ready right now to perform a heroic deed
Of unprecedented prowess for your sake
I am ready to conceal my feelings to please you
I am ready to do anything for your sake
Not only to be a husband, but a servant.

Editing a song, providing just enough to give the audience a feel for the moment, is always an option. But in this case, the lyrics foreshadow upcoming events and speak directly to Lee's feelings for Marina, which suggests that the selection from the song should be sung or spoken in its entirety.

As for "*as he gets on his knees, caressing her feet,*" the phrase could be added to the newly revised stage direction before the aria so it reads, "*Softly, in Russian, LEE sings some of an aria from 'The Queen of Spades' as he gets on his knees, caressing her feet.*" Lee can sing the aria softly, so that adverb can be cut. If the actor does not sing or speak Russian, the revised stage direction would read, "*In Russian, LEE sings some of an aria from 'The Queen of Spades' as he caresses her feet.*"

But caressing Marina's feet would look strange in a Reading, and occupy both Lee's hands. If the actors approve, Lee could stroke Marina's hair or put his arm around her while the phrase "*caressing her feet*" is read. But this is not essential information and can be eliminated. Thus, if the actor playing Lee speaks the lines from the aria softly in English and strokes Marina's hair, the revised stage direction, "*In Russian, LEE sings some of an aria from 'The Queen of Spades,'*" will have solved all of the challenges.

Unconventional Stage Directions

Playwrights should write stage directions however they like, and many playwrights choose to write stage directions that are unconventional when judged by traditional standards. These stage directions are often less prescriptive and more inventive. They may provide information about location, action, or emotional content, but they do so in unusual ways. They can spark imagination.

Novelistic and Poetic

Unconventional stage directions come in various styles. Some are novelistic, with long, descriptive passages. Others are poetic or abstract. Still others may require unusual behavior from the cast. In all these cases, the voice of the writer is revealed more conspicuously than in conventional stage directions.

> *Paula Vogel, I'll never forget, in a class at Brown, sat us down and she read the first stage directions from a Tennessee Williams play. And Paula said, "these aren't stage directions, these are a love letter from Tennessee Williams to his reader, over time." I thought, "Oh God, that's right." So Paula really gave me permission to think of them in a different way—to not think of them as blocking or props [. . .] but to think of them a little bit more abstractly, and a little bit more in a readerly way. You're communicating with a reader. Maybe your first reader is an actor who will be in the play, or a designer, or maybe just someone who likes to read plays— which aren't usually very fun to read—but there would be an intimacy of contact with a reader. I don't think I do it consciously, but if I had to be conscious about it, that's what I would say.*
>
> Sarah Ruhl, Playwright

What should the artistic team do with these various types of unconventional stage directions in a Play Reading?

Novelistic stage directions evoke the ambience of the play for which they are written. While they often provide pertinent information, they go further, offering descriptions replete with images and detail. Hearing these stage directions can be satisfying in a Reading, as they are usually crafted with considerable skill.

If the director chooses to incorporate novelistic stage directions, the suggestions offered previously for editing traditional stage directions apply. The dramatic impact of a Reading can be hindered if an audience is required to listen to extensive stage directions despite their qualities as literature. Any stage direction that includes important information should be read, and perhaps those that capture the voice of the writer most precisely. Unless the attempt with the Reading is to create an entirely unique event and not to suggest a production of the play, careful, conscientious editing of novelistic stage directions is worthwhile.

Poetic or abstract stage directions may inspire the creative team. These stage directions are often written for "alternative" plays. Writers of plot and character-driven plays rarely incorporate abstract stage directions, which take time to analyze and consider. Play Readings, like all theatrical experiences, exist in time. Audiences at Readings are not at liberty to ponder the meaning of oblique stage directions. Given their complexity, nearly all abstract stage directions, which are usually nonessential, can be eliminated. However, playwrights and directors may decide that some of the most tantalizingly abstract or poetic stage directions remain, providing a glimpse of the writer's style.

Unusual Behavior

Other stage directions are atypical in that they require unusual behavior from the actors. Examples of this type are found in "Samara." (See Appendix G.) Below is a scene from the play as written:

Scene Eight

Clinic *CRAIG leans over SURAIYA, who lies prostrate in a chair, in the midst of an ultrasound. The DOCTOR controls the ultrasound.*

DOCTOR And . . . ohp. Ohp! There we go. There it is.

CRAIG watches as the lights brighten a different part of the stage to reveal AMIT. He is a fully-grown Indian man, about the same age as SURAIYA, even though he is in reality just an amorphous blob.

CRAIG Wow. See that, Suraiya?

SURAIYA Yes. "Wow."

AMIT gets up, moves to the doctor's office. Only SURAIYA sees him.

AMIT Hi.

SURAIYA tries to ignore him, as CRAIG stares at the monitor. AMIT taps her on the shoulder. She doesn't respond. AMIT taps harder.

SURAIYA What.

AMIT I said hi.

SURAIYA I heard.

AMIT And you?

SURAIYA Yes?

AMIT Wellll.

SURAIYA Well what?

AMIT What do you say?

SURAIYA *(relents)* Hi.

AMIT What're they doing?

SURAIYA They're looking at you.

AMIT Yeah?

SURAIYA Yep.

CRAIG Well, can you tell the—gender?

DOCTOR Of course!

CRAIG Well . . . ?

DOCTOR I can tell you, but I can't *really* tell you—

CRAIG Oh. Right.

CRAIG hands the DOCTOR some money.

DOCTOR *(confidentially)* It's a boy!

```
CRAIG It's a boy?
AMIT I'm a boy!
SURAIYA (unenthused) You're a boy.
CRAIG runs off.
CRAIG A boy!
AMIT magically sprouts male characteristics.
```

Craig and Katie, an American couple, have conceived a child with Suraiya, a surrogate from India. The play is not a naturalistic treatment of this subject. Many scenes take place in the characters' imaginations. With nontraditional plays such as this, the playwright and director should work together to discuss how the action described in the stage directions for each scene will be presented in the Reading before any edits are made. Below are suggestions as to how the stage directions in "Samsara" can be revised and enacted in ways that take the audience on the play's whimsical journey.

Amit, the fetus in "Samsara," is a fully developed character who interacts with his "mother" from the moment of his conception. The audience should know that in the fanciful world of the play, only Suraiya sees and interacts with Amit. To communicate this, the stage direction should be revised so that the Doctor, along with Craig, watches the monitor.

```
CRAIG watches and the DOCTOR watch the monitor as
    the lights brighten a different part of the
    stage to reveal AMIT.
```

As Craig and the Doctor watch the fetus on the monitor, the actor playing Amit, *"a fully-grown Indian man,"* moves from retreat position to an assigned music stand when he is referenced. Craig and the Doctor stare at the monitor as Suraiya looks directly at Amit. Notice that while the other characters are standing, Suriaya is seated on a stool, suggesting the stage direction *"lies prostrate in a chair"*(see Photograph 9.20).

```
CRAIG watches and the DOCTOR watch the monitor
    as the lights brighten a different part of
    the stage to reveal AMIT. He is a fully-
    grown Indian man, about the same age as
    SURAIYA, even though he is in reality just an
    amorphous blob.
```

It might be useful to break up the stage direction, giving Suraiya a moment to notice Amit.

```
CRAIG and the DOCTOR watch the monitor as the
    lights brighten a different part of the stage
    to reveal AMIT. He is a fully-grown Indian
    man, about the same age as SURAIYA.
```

The reader resumes after Suraiya notices Amit:

```
Even though he is in reality just an amorphous
    blob.
```

Photograph 9.20

Photograph 9.21

The audience may need to be reminded that Amit is a fetus, so that phrase should not be cut. But how might Amit react to hearing himself described as *"an amorphous blob"*? Amit's subsequent behavior suggests he would not appreciate this description, in which case he could react to the stage directions reader. This is an unusual notion for a Reading befitting an unusual play.

A reader in a play with surprising stage directions such as those in "Samsara" as well as plays with novelistic or abstract stage directions can function as a proxy for the playwright's voice. The stage directions readers are not characters in the plays, but their active participation in Readings responds stylistically to how these writers use stage directions.

The artistic team can determine behavior or a gesture that best conveys Amit's attitude when this stage direction is read. This should be comic, suited to the tone of the play (see Photograph 9.21).

Or, given that he is fully grown, Amit could execute a conspicuously adult gesture. Options abound. But the curious stage direction *"Even though he is in reality just an amorphous blob"* encourages a reaction from the actor playing Amit. Bringing the stage direction reader into the action reflects the imaginative world of the play.

> CRAIG Wow. See that, Suraiya?
> SURAIYA Yes. "Wow."
> *AMIT gets up, moves to the doctor's office. Only*
> *SURAIYA sees him.*

If the actor playing Amit moves to the music stand next to Suraiya and she watches him while Craig and the Doctor focus on the monitor, the stage direction can be cut.

> ~~*AMIT gets up, moves to the doctor's office. Only*~~
> ~~*SURAIYA sees him.*~~

But since the reader has been recruited into the action, she might want to watch the events unfold (see Photo 9.22).

> AMIT Hi.
> *SURAIYA tries to ignore him, as CRAIG stares at*
> *the monitor. AMIT taps her on the shoulder.*
> *She doesn't respond. AMIT taps harder.*

Suraiya can turn away from Amit, and he can tap her on the shoulder and then tap harder, so the entire stage direction is struck (see Photograph 9.23).

> ~~*SURAIYA tries to ignore him, as CRAIG stares at*~~
> ~~*the monitor. AMIT taps her on the shoulder.*~~
> ~~*She doesn't respond. AMIT taps harder.*~~
> SURAIYA What.
> AMIT I said hi.
> SURAIYA I heard.
> AMIT And you?
> SURAIYA Yes?

Photograph 9.22

Photograph 9.23

```
AMIT Wellll.
SURAIYA Well what?
AMIT What do you say?
SURAIYA (relents) Hi.
```

Amit should look at the Doctor and Craig before he says the next line.

```
AMIT What're they doing?
SURAIYA They're looking at you.
AMIT Yeah?
SURAIYA Yep.
CRAIG Can you tell the—gender?
DOCTOR Of course!
CRAIG Well . . . ?
DOCTOR I can tell you, but I can't really tell you—
CRAIG Oh. Right.
CRAIG hands the DOCTOR some money.
```

That Craig needs to pay the Doctor to learn the child's gender is peculiar, so the stage direction should be read. The Doctor can gesture to suggest that he is requesting payment, and Craig's move suggests that he is taking money out his wallet (see Photograph 9.24). Then Craig hands the Doctor the money (see Photograph 9.25). Notice that in photographs 9.24 and 9.25, Craig's and the Doctor's hands are positioned above or between the music stands, in full view of the audience, and Suraiya's and Amit's hands are also visible and revealing. This is an advantage of using music stands for Readings.

```
DOCTOR (confidentially) It's a boy!
CRAIG It's a boy?
AMIT I'm a boy!
SURAIYA (unenthused) You're a boy.
CRAIG runs off.
CRAIG A boy!
DOCTOR (confidentially) It's a boy!
CRAIG It's a boy?
AMIT I'm a boy!
SURAIYA (unenthused) You're a boy.
CRAIG runs off.
CRAIG A boy!
```

Given that he has another line, Craig could run off later; either way, the stage direction is excised. However, we are venturing into uncharted territory with the next stage direction:

```
AMIT magically sprouts male characteristics.
```

The event described is unusual, to say the least; like many unconventional stage directions, it can invigorate the artists involved with a full production. If this stage direction were cut for the Reading, the audience would lose important information. But reading the stage direction without some sort of physical adjustment

Photograph 9.24

Photograph 9.25

Photograph 9.26

from Amit might squander a comic opportunity. As for what that gesture might be, the possibilities are as limitless as the creative team's imaginations (see Photograph 9.26).

Readings of plays with quirky stage directions pose risks and rewards for playwrights, directors and actors. Choosing which stage directions to read helps an audience access the writer's vision. Gestures and physical adjustments can reveal the distinct world of the play. The role of the stage directions reader may venture into the realm of concept. Unless the playwright prefers not to be involved, the creative approach to the Reading should be decided upon by the playwright and director in advance and adapted in rehearsal with input from the cast.

By incorporating the playwright's voice through the selective use of novelistic, poetic, abstract, or unusual stage directions, Readings of these types of plays are distinct from the full productions, almost as if there were another character in the play. The casting choice for the stage directions reader is vital. But no clear guide exists for presenting Readings of plays with anomalous stage directions. Each one is unique.

CHAPTER 10

REVIEW AND INCORPORATING TECHNICAL CUES

The limited rehearsal period for a Play Reading must be used effectively. Technical elements such as lighting and sound cues should be limited. Actors need a one-hour break at minimum between the end of rehearsal and the start of the Reading. Taking a break is not optional—it is essential.

If the director is using light or sound, time must be allotted to incorporate these elements with the actors either during the stop-and-go or after the rehearsal and before the break. If time allows, cues that were set in the stop-and-go can be reviewed.

Before the Break

- Set the stage wash and any internal light cues for the Reading.
- Review or incorporate music and sound effects.
- Set sound enhancement levels.
- Check voice projection.
- Stage or review the entrances, bows, and exits.
- Review any challenging scenes.
- Remove all personal belongings from the playing area and the venue.
- Set water bottles for the cast under retreat position chairs. Be sure that the bottles are not noisy or crinkly.
- Remind actors not to bring their pencils onstage.

For some Readings, directors have full access to lighting and sound equipment, and a stage manager. Before the day of rehearsal, the director asked if the producer allowed sound and light cues and if technical support was provided. If allowed, the director either sends the sound cues in advance or brings them to rehearsal, per the stage manager's request.

Lighting

Because rehearsals often take place under different lighting than the Reading itself—usually house lights or work lights—a specific light cue should be set for the Reading. In many cases, this "stage wash" is the only light cue.

All actors should be present to determine the level of this cue. The intensity must be consistent across the playing area, including the reader's music stand. To set the wash, actors should be certain they can read the script at each of their assigned music stands and when the music stands are raised, lowered, and angled. The director surveys the cue from the house so that the wash is uniform: The actors at either end of the semicircle should be lit as fully as the actors center stage. Everyone needs enough light to read the scripts. The cue is determined by the actor who needs the most light.

Clip-on music stand lights are used for some Readings. Unless they were incorporated in rehearsal, they should be tested before the Reading to be sure they provide enough light. Directors should also determine who will turn on each light and when. The easiest option is for the director or stage manager to turn on all the music stand lights before the audience enters or for the first actor at each stand to turn on the light. The last actor to use each clip-on light can turn it off.

The wash for actors in retreat positions should also be set. If possible, this cue should be darker than at the cue at the music stands, but bright enough for the actors to see the scripts. A uniform level is best for retreat positions, again determined by the actor who needs the most light.

Directors may want the lighting for the Reading to be atmospheric. This is fine if the lights are bright enough for all of the actors to read the scripts effortlessly.

Internal Light Cues

Internal light cues take time to "tech." They are not necessary for most Readings. If the director decides that internal cues are important for a few scenes, such as a blackout or an "isolation cue" (which narrows the focus to a few actors), these cues should be set with the stage manager and actors before the break. Cues that were incorporated in the stop-and-go can be reviewed.

Blackouts are not required for Readings; that said, a blackout cue at the act break or an important moment in the play can be effective. If the Reading includes blackouts, they should be set and rehearsed with all of the actors in their exact positions. Actors should not move or exit during blackouts in a Reading. After a few moments, the wash can be restored, allowing the actors to move or exit safely.

The stage manager and director should set the level of the house lights for when the audience enters and decide when this cue will transition into the stage wash for each act of the Reading. If possible, these transitional cues should be set with the actors, but if time is running short, as is often the case, house light levels and transitional cues can be set during the break.

The stage wash will warm the venue and the playing area. The director and stage manager, and in some cases a house manager, should be sure that the room temperature is comfortable for the audience and the actors.

Music, Sound Effects, and Enhancement Mics

Play Readings do not need internal music cues or sound effects. Stage directions referencing music or sound can be read. It is easier for the reader to say *"We hear a crash"* or *"We hear Ella Fitzgerald sing 'How High the Moon'"* than to cue and set levels. It is also possible for the stage directions reader or the actor to execute certain sound cues, for example, knocking on the music stand to suggest a knock on the door. The choice is determined by the specific cues, the number of cues, the function they perform in the play, and the length of the rehearsal period.

That said, even if the venue does not have a technical booth, incorporating a few sound cues into a Play Reading using an iPod docking station, a laptop computer or CD player is relatively easy. It is the director's responsibility to provide the stage manager with either CDs or MP3s. The cues should be incorporated or reviewed with the actors before the break. Volume levels should be precise for cues that underscore spoken dialogue. During rehearsal and performance, the stage manager, the director, or an assistant can run the cues.

Music that accompanies entrances and exit may be worthwhile. Carefully chosen music can help establish the period and the tone of a play and add a flourish to the beginning and end of a Reading. The music could accompany the entrance of the actors and fade out when they are in position.

With the exception of certain musicals, most Readings are performed without microphones. Attaching wireless body mics and mic packs to the actors should be avoided if at all possible: If not, time must be allocated. Microphones can also be attached to music stands. If so, time should be allowed to tech these mics.

For Readings performed in large venues, the use of enhancement microphones such as floor mics or hanging mics is more common than body mics. Enhancement mics should be located so that they amplify the actors' voices without requiring actors to be in specific positions. If enhancement mics require specific actor placement, the director should know in advance and position the actors accordingly. A volume level for any type of enhancement mic should be set with the actors before the break. While body mics and enhancement mics increase the volume level, they do not rectify slurred diction—they will only make it louder.

Play Readings pose challenges for voice projection. Actors look down at the scripts rather than face up as they would in production. They likely have not been using their full voices at rehearsal. Actors need to be attentive to diction and to voice projection whether enhancement mics are used or not. By their very presence, even the most attentive audiences make noise. Actors need to compensate.

Directors should take a few minutes to check voice projection, as the acoustics in every venue are different and may be deceptive. The director can stand at the back of the venue toward the end of rehearsal and ask the actors to read a few lines from the script exactly as they will be doing soon in front of the audience. This is time well spent. While most actors will instinctively project in performance, nothing is more frustrating to audiences—and playwrights—than when they cannot hear the actors.

Entrances, Initial Positions, Intermission, Bows, and Exits

Before the break, the director should determine how the actors will enter the playing area. The choice is informed by the particulars of the venue, the policies of the producing organization, and the preference of the director. Actors should not wander into the venue at random for a public Play Reading except in very informal settings or when the play suggests such an approach.

In most cases, actors enter single file in an order determined by their first assigned positions. It may be necessary to rehearse the entrance more than once. A sloppy entrance does not portend well for a Play Reading.

Directors may decide that actors move directly to their assigned positions for the first scene, with some actors positioned at music stands and others in retreat positions. Or they may prefer that the entire cast is in retreat positions when the reader first speaks. Once the actors are positioned, the stage directions reader states the name of the play, the name of the playwright, and, in some cases, the name of the director. For most plays, information about the setting is also read. The actor with the first line should know the specific cue.

If the actors in the first scene moved to their assigned positions upon entering, when the reader is done, the actor with the first line can begin speaking. If the cast began in retreat positions, the actors in the first scene can move to assigned music stands after the opening stage directions are read. If the opening stage directions include characters' names, each actor could move to his or her position when their character is referenced.

The reader could also introduce all of the characters by name with a brief description as that actor moves to an assigned music stand or acknowledges simply that he or she is portraying the referenced character. This works well for large-cast plays. Whatever the choice, a well-executed entrance for the cast and an orderly approach to the top of the Reading are essential.

If there will be an intermission, the exit for the act break should be rehearsed with the same attention to detail. When the reader says *"End of Act One"* and the audience applauds, the actors exit single file.

Many two-act plays can be performed without intermission in a Reading. If the presentation will run an hour and forty-five minutes or less, intermission can be eliminated unless the playwright, director, or any of the actors feel it is necessary. Given that with many Readings, the first time the play is performed without stopping is in front of the audience, the director and playwright may need to approximate the running time. If the producing organization allows, the decision about whether or not to take an intermission can be made after rehearsal and announced to the audience before the Reading. If there is an intermission, the cast should also rehearse their entrance for the top of the second act. Directors should not leave entrances and exits to chance.

Some Play Readings are presented without curtain calls or final bows. This is a mistake. Audiences expect them, and actors deserve them. Only in a very casual setting would a public Reading be presented without a company bow. Also, actors should wait to gather their scripts and to chat with one another until the audience has finished applauding.

Final bows for Readings do not need to be as elaborate as they might be in production. A company bow will suffice. The stage directions reader joins the cast for the bow. The director can decide if the actors will join hands. A designated actor should lead the company bow and, so there is no confusion, hold to lead a second bow if the audience continues to applaud. Given that the playing area may be crowded with music stands, the director can place the curtain call behind the stands or in front of them. Whatever the choice, final bows for Readings should be rehearsed.

After the bow, actors exit the playing area. In informal settings, actors can step off of the stage and mingle with friends. If a talkback is scheduled, a short break after the Reading ends and before the talkback begins is mandatory.

Memorization

Some actors will attempt to memorize entire sections of the script before a Play Reading. This is counterproductive. While the impulse is admirable, actors should remember that they are, in fact, performing in a Reading. Familiarity with the lines is required, but memorization is not. Also, given that the other actors have not committed the scene to memory, the presentation will feel imbalanced from the audience's perspective. As with under-rehearsed blocking, partial memorization can weaken the performance rather than enhance it.

> *I always remind actors not to apologize for reading the text. It's okay to look down at the script. Together in rehearsal, we'll find moments where they can look up.*
>
> Daniella Topol, Director

Some directors may request that certain lines or parts of scenes are memorized, but this should be done selectively. Directors should never insist that actors memorize lines; actors have the final say. However, a few memorized lines, mutually agreed upon by the director and the cast, may come in handy.

Useful Memorization

- During a scene involving a violence or physical intimacy, when actors may need to use both of their hands
- A key line or exchange of dialogue, for example, the last few lines of the play
- When an actor is crossing to another music stand, to maintain the pace of a scene.

Any scene involving memorized lines should be rehearsed more than once. If an actor has any difficulty with memorizing the requested lines, the director should not persist. Memorization should never be required.

Reviewing Scenes and Beats

After setting and reviewing any technical cues and staging the entrances, exits, and bows, the artistic team can review challenging scenes or beats. Everyone on the team should have a say in what will be reviewed. The choice must be selective. Rare indeed is a Play Reading rehearsal with time to spare, and likely, only the most essential beats can be reviewed. After soliciting input, directors and playwrights should have final say.

What to Review

- Scenes involving considerable movement
- Scenes requiring a brisk tempo
- Scenes involving violence or intimacy
- Scenes incorporating props
- Scenes, beats, or lines with pronunciation demands
- The opening and closing beats of the play
- Any memorized lines
- Any other challenging beats as determined by the playwright, director, or actors.

Making effective use of remaining time is crucial for a Play Reading. While the entire creative team would like every moment in the play to be perfectly articulated, they should trust that many of their concerns will be resolved in performance, and something may be learned from those that are not. Also, unless it is critical, for example, if an actor is inaudible, directors should refrain from giving notes during intermission.

A Reading captures a new work at a specific moment in time. It is a step on the developmental path of the play that may lead to a full production, the final stage of development.

CHAPTER 11

ACTING IN A PLAY READING

Most of the qualities that make for an effective performance by an actor in a full production apply to Play Readings. But Readings require actors to adapt their approaches to accommodate limited rehearsal periods. Some actors do this effortlessly. For others, the experience is frustrating. Given the prominence of Play Readings in contemporary theatre, actors who wish to be involved with new plays need to either embrace the challenges or learn to work effectively within them. For emerging actors, developing the skills to perform in a Play Reading is imperative.

Readings can provide career opportunities. Actors who are involved in one or more Readings of a play during its development have a foot in the door of the full production. Even if they do not continue with the play, Readings provide actors with opportunities to collaborate with playwrights, producers, directors, even the literary staff, and let these people see their work.

Actors in Readings

I love actors who do readings. I know they are looking for opportunity but they can also be so selfless and giving. I've known some actors to do two or three readings a week. They know that they probably won't go the distance to production because they don't have "star" value, but they do them anyway. Many believe it is not only part of their job, but that they have a responsibility to developing the art form. We'd be in tough shape without their contribution.
David Esbjornsen, Director

There's something "holy" about a reading whose main objective is helping the playwright develop her work. There's an embrace and respect for the artists in the room. People care. And then it doesn't really matter if I get cast down the line.
Susan Louise O'Connor, Actor

A Play Reading is not a showcase for an actor. With most Readings, the writer is still discovering the play. If a character's motivation is vague, a playwright may learn that from an actor. Playwrights benefit most when actors do what they can with the material they are given, letting writers hear what is working and what is not.

The best way to learn how to perform effectively in Play Readings is through experience. There is now a generation of actors who have performed in countless Readings. They refine and adjust their training methods to work within the parameters. They analyze scripts and interpret characters with minimal elucidation from directors or playwrights. An element of improvisation informs their performances. Many actors embrace the opportunity, fully aware that the approach has little to do with the detailed exploration of character for a full production.

Before Rehearsal

Actors should study the script in advance of rehearsal and decide on clear objectives for their character. Tentative, hesitant tactics hold back Readings.

> *Even with a table read, I expect the actors to familiarize themselves with the script in advance. It's disrespectful of the playwright to come in totally cold.*
>
> Caridad Svich, Playwright

If they have printed out a copy of the script or Reading draft, actors should highlight their lines. If they have important questions they would like answered before rehearsal, they can email the director. Most actors are cast because their work is respected, and someone connected with the play believes they are right for the role. Actors should trust their abilities.

Certain scripts require an actor to sing, to speak with an accent, to speak lines in a foreign language, or to pronounce difficult or obscure words. Actors can explore these elements on their own; however, they should consult with the director to see how these moments will be handled in rehearsal.

> *I prefer to write questions down and ask them at rehearsal, rather than email them before. The answers may be helpful to everyone in the room. At rehearsal, I like to hear from the director and playwright what the big events of the play are, and how the cast can help lift them up. I also like to know if the playwright has questions. It's fine if the directors decide in advance at which music stands the actors will be placed, but most of the time, it's obvious. It's more fun if the actors in the room are involved in the decisions, and given the freedom to be open with suggestions.*
>
> Susan Louise O'Connor, Actor

During Rehearsal

Actors bring a highlighter and a pencil to rehearsal. They note in their scripts any changes in stage directions made during rehearsal. They may also need to write the pronunciation of difficult words phonetically. Any notes, cues, or rewrites should be written clearly in their scripts so they can be referenced easily during performance.

Unless they are discouraged from doing so by the director, actors in Play Readings should get their characters into their bodies. Physicalization is more challenging when actors are seated; nonetheless, actors on chairs and stools should strive to keep their bodies alive with character-specific physical choices. That said, there are ways in which physicality is modified for Readings. Gestures that might be fully extended in performance are better if suggested in Readings.

Pacing for most Play Readings is often quicker than for full productions. With no production elements to assist in telling the story, the focus is exclusively on the text, and pauses suggest that an actor has dropped a cue.

When a playwright or director feels that an actor's choice is not effective and suggests something different, the actor should adapt, even if he or she disagrees. The actor may be right, but the Reading will determine that. While asking pertinent questions may be useful, offering suggestions for rewrites to the playwright, unless specifically solicited, is not.

In general, actors in Play Reading need to be open, willing collaborators and sensitive to the singular purpose of the Reading: to serve the writer.

> *Simply, it is not my purpose to rewrite the play.*
>
> Lynn Cohen, Actor

Actors who perform frequently in Play Readings become remarkably adept at picking up cue lines, maintaining the rhythm and pace, finding opportunities to look up from the script, and making eye contact. They are able to do all of this without paraphrasing or missing their cues. For many audiences, this is what brings a Reading to life.

Looking up Made Easy

- Actors should familiarize themselves with their lines before rehearsal.
- The font size of the reading draft can be slightly larger than normal (14 point rather than 12 point). It is appropriate for an actor to request a larger font size; however, the font size should be uniform in all of the scripts so page numbers can be easily referenced in rehearsal
- Actors should highlight their lines in the scripts. They should use a light-colored highlighter, or their scripts may be difficult to read.
- Actors should manipulate all of the music stands when they arrive for rehearsal.
- Actors should raise or lower the music stands every time they relocate, if need be. Music stands should be positioned at a height which allows the actors to glance down at the script to read their lines and easily look up at their fellow actors.
- With the director's approval, actors can angle their music stands toward the actors to whom they are speaking.

Monologues and Cue Phrases

Scenes that contain monologues or lengthy speeches can be difficult for Reading audiences. Monologues require an actor to look down at the script for an extended time. If the actor is alone onstage, the director and actor might locate a few moments where the actor can look up from the script. These will result in pauses, and should be done only when interpretively sound.

If other actors are in the scene, they should give their focus to the actor delivering the monologue throughout. The actor reading the monologue may find suitable moments to look up at these actors. To be certain he or she does not miss a cue, the actor who has the next line in the scene can highlight a few words—a "cue phrase"—toward the end of the monologue. When the monologue begins, the actor with the next line can glance at the cue phrase. When the cue phrase is spoken, the actor looks back at the script. Highlighting a cue phrase prevents an unnecessary pause. Although many actors do this on their own, directors can suggest cue phrases.

Actors listening to the monologue can also make minor physical adjustments to convey their reactions to what they are hearing. Modifications such as these allow the audience to be more fully engaged in a scene with a monologue than if all of the actors are looking down at their scripts.

Stage Directions Reader

The person who reads stage directions should be an individual with stage presence and a strong speaking voice. This is a point on which there is almost universal consensus.

Actors as Readers

Who should read stage directions is a more critical question than one might think at first blush. I had a couple of experiences early on in which the theatre producing the reading had a staff member approach me and suggest that I use a stage manager to read the stage directions. Each time I agreed to this it was, at best, neutral and, at worst, disastrous. I soon stopped agreeing to such suggestions. This is nothing against stage managers, but reading stage directions well should not be expected to occur naturally within their skill set.

The stage directions reader must be someone who is a good storyteller, someone who is sensitive to what is going on in the room, who rides rhythms and energies that are happening in the moment and who has a range of colors with which he or she paints words. In other words, you need an actor.

You want the stage directions to move you smoothly through a moment, conjuring what the audience needs to understand. In addition, the stage directions reader serves as a sort of motor that keeps the momentum of a reading going. Not that you want this person to rush, but there is often an opportunity to build excitement and anticipation as to what the next scene might hold.

Technically, they must never allow pauses to creep in before their stage directions within a scene. Such pauses are death to the momentum and flow of a reading. The exception to the pause rule will

> *generally happen at the end of a scene when you may want that last*
> *moment to hang in the air before wiping the slate clean with a nicely*
> *punctuating, "Scene."*
>   *It can be challenging to find solid actors willing to read stage*
> *directions. Although they're a very important part of a successful*
> *reading, it can be seen as a bit of a thankless job. That said, there are*
> *many young and hungry performers looking for the opportunity to get a*
> *foot in the door at a theatre, or to work with the director or playwright.*
> *Sometimes it's useful to let the actor know just how important the job is*
> *(which is the truth), and that you thought of them specifically because*
> *of the skills they would bring to bear on the enterprise.*
>
> Will Pomerantz, Director

Reading stage directions inaudibly or tentatively, stumbling over words, stepping on actors' lines, or waiting too long to speak will undermine the quality of the Reading.

Stage direction readers should examine their lines in the Reading draft as conscientiously as the actors. They should carefully note in their scripts any changes that are made during rehearsal. If a stage direction is substantially revised, the director should allow the readers the time needed to rewrite it in its entirety. Directors should take the readers' responsibilities seriously and give them notes just as they give notes to actors.

In most cases, the stage directions reader should look down at the script throughout the Play Reading. When they look at the actors, the audience's response can be influenced by the readers' reactions. Readers would not be onstage during the production: They are not part of the audience and should not respond to the play as if they were. The stage directions reader should not be a "stand-in" for the audience.

Readers should attend all rehearsals. They inform the rhythm and tempo of the play. It can damage the Reading if the director, out of courtesy, allows the reader to arrive late. If the reader cannot attend, the director, playwright, or stage manager should make note of all changes in stage directions as well as any visual or timing cues that were decided in rehearsal that would affect when a stage direction is read and review these with the reader before the performance.

The reader, may also perform a small role in the play. Directors can help stage directions readers distinguish between their function as reader and any character they portray by establishing a clear visual convention. When a reader goes into character, he or she can stand, move to an unattended music stand, or change the position of their music stand. If this move is accompanied by a character-specific physical adjustment, the audience will understand that the reader has entered the world of the play.

In England, the general practice is for the director to read stage directions. This approach has its advantages. Directors can inform and even control the tone and tempo of Readings. If the pace is dragging, they can accelerate their line readings. If actors are too quiet, directors can talk louder. Directors-as-readers can speak soothingly if the actors are too intense. Directors who read stage directions can direct by example.

However, when directors also serve as readers, they cannot see and hear the Reading objectively nor assess the response as effectively as when they are sitting among the audience. Moreover, not all directors are good readers. In the United States, directors rarely read stage directions. They can observe and evaluate the Reading, but once the performance is underway, the actors are on their own.

CHAPTER 12

DEVELOPMENT AND PRESENTATION

Process versus Product

At any stage of development for a new play or musical, the artistic team may be faced with a challenging question: To what degree is the future of the piece determined by the quality of the presentation?

While Play Readings are developmental steps, the process of working on them is not, in and of itself, developmental. There is not enough time for rewrites. The creative team examines the current draft of the material and focuses on the performance.

At many organizations, unless the piece has already been slated for production, a Reading is, in effect, an audition—for the actors, for the writers, for the director, and for the piece itself. That Readings often serve as auditions is the unspoken rule of new play development. Opportunities for further development or production are influenced and, in some cases, determined by the quality of the presentation.

With this awareness, should the creative team spend the rehearsal period on developing the piece or crafting a quality presentation? Are rehearsals about the process or the product? These contradictory impulses affect how the time is used. When more time is offered, as discussed below, the "process versus product" dilemma becomes more pronounced. This is the case for Staged Readings and Workshops of musicals and operas as well as plays.

Presentation as Pitch

One of the downsides of this model is that at the end of the workshop, the presentation has to feel like a performance—like some kind of show. We have to balance using the workshop for development vs. using it as a "pitch." The anticipation and acknowledgement of presentation is a given with this model. So if we have a five-day rehearsal period, the first three days are development, and the last two days are to prepare for the pitch. At the presentation I'll say, "Welcome to our last rehearsal. Here's what to pay attention to and what not to pay attention to."

Dan Fields, Creative Director, Walt Disney
Imagineering Creative Entertainment

We do readings for two opposing reasons: to contribute to the devel-opment of new writing/support writers in their process, and to deter-mine which plays we want to produce. Knowing that the readings are used to make programming decisions may discourage the writers from taking risks. But the process lets us know if a writer is flexible.

Nick Connaughton, Creative Entertainment
Manager, Arcola Theatre

The opera workshop presentations are always for donors, company members, even press. This is to generate enthusiasm about the piece, but it sometimes creates a conflict between process and product. So I spend the first part of the workshop concentrating on process, and the last few days is about product.

Kevin Newbury, Director

Unless they are specifically told that the process and presentation are entirely for developmental purposes, playwrights, directors, and actors often proceed under the assumption that any Reading or Workshop may decide the future of the piece with that organization. And in some cases, the quality of their work may determine their future involvement.

Additional Rehearsal Time

When producers offer additional rehearsal time, they should make their expecta-tions clear to the creative team. Should the time be spent on development, or do the producers expect to see a polished performance at the end of the rehearsal period?

Developmental labs and certain theatres are writer-oriented. Their interest is in the playwright more than the specific play. This is clearly communicated to the writers by the leaders of these organizations. Most labs are highly competitive, but when a playwright is accepted into one of their programs, the artistic team is free to work in whatever way the playwright chooses.

At the Playwrights' Center, we are playwright-centric. Our obli-gation is to the writers. Our mission is to support playwrights—getting an audience excited is not our main focus, though we have cultivated an audience around the readings that appreciates see-ing new work in development. Playwrights can work on what-ever they want. They determine the approach. They choose their collaborators. Nothing is forced on them. As for the degree of staging—it's up to the playwrights. Talkbacks—up to the play-wrights. Everything we do is for the playwrights' benefit. We prefer longer rehearsal periods, and workshops. Too short an amount of time limits what can be accomplished.

Hayley Finn, Associate Artistic Director,
Playwright's Center, Minneapolis

When producers encourage artists to use the time for development, the future of the piece and their involvement is not at stake. In these situations, playwrights should decide the approach. Writers may throw out a few scenes entirely and replace them with new ones. They may add a character or kill one off. With the director's assistance, a writer may encourage actors to attack certain scenes differently. They can experiment with alternate endings. Challenges unique to the piece might be explored. If the play contains violence, a fight choreographer might work with the actors. Dialects, accents, and heightened language could be examined.

When offered additional time for development, while the first impulse might be to experiment, one of the most effective strategies is in many ways the simplest: table work. The playwright, director, and actors can dig deeper into the text—scrutinize scenes, characters, relationships, events, rhythm, tone, and style. All of the questions prohibited by the limited rehearsal period for a Reading can be fully explored. A concentrated investigation of the script can be of great use to writers.

Playwrights could also divide up how they use the additional time. They can explore the play with the director and actors at table for a few days and then spend a day or two with the actors on their feet. Writers can take a day off in between to work on rewrites. There is no template for how the time can be used when the creative team is given free rein.

However, when some producers offer more time, they expect to see a performance that will allow them to make a decision about whether or not to move forward with the piece. If this is the case, the director—and perhaps designers—could generate a ground plan. The staging for the entire piece could be sketched out. Music stands would be replaced with rehearsal furniture, and many or all stage directions eliminated. With a musical, a few of the dance numbers could be fully staged. The cast might memorize a few scenes. The specific approach would be determined by the amount of time offered, but all of the artists involved are clear that product is the goal.

When additional rehearsal time is provided, the decision about how to use the time is determined by the expectations of the producers. If they want to see a "pitch" for production, the quality of the presentation is crucial.

Whom to Invite When

In commercial theatre, make sure you have the best possible material before inviting potential investors, or anyone who can make decisions about the future of the show.

Cara Reichel, Producing Artistic Director,
Prospect Theater Company

Make sure you know the show is what you want it to be before you invite anyone important to a reading. If it doesn't go well, getting them to come back is hard. It may not be smart to invite important industry people to a first reading of something; you may have no idea of how it plays if you have never seen it in front of an audience

before. Invite friends and colleagues early in development for feed-back. And don't send the piece out if it's not done; what's the rush?
James Morgan, Producing Artistic Director,
York Theatre Company

Picking an audience is as important as picking the director and the cast. Who you invite to a reading depends on the purpose of the reading. Knowing what the reading is for is essential. Is it a backer's audition, for agents or producers? Is it for civilians, who replicate the target audience? Who you invite also depends on the venue. If your goal is to hear the play for rewrites, than any venue is fine. But if your goal is to invite potential backers, then you need to present the reading in a place where backers will come.
Ralph Sevush, Esq., Executive Director/Business and
Legal Affairs, Dramatists Guild of America, Inc.

█████████

CHAPTER 13

DEVELOPING NEW MUSICALS AND OPERAS

The proliferation of Readings is not limited to straight plays. With increasing frequency, new musicals and operas travel through a number of developmental steps before production, from In-house Readings of the book or libretto to partially or fully staged Workshops. While many of the same guidelines for Play Reading apply, because of all the components—and the expense—developing musicals and operas impose additional demands.

The York Theatre Company, Prospect Theater Company, The BMI Lehman Engel Musical Theater Workshop, and Walt Disney Imagineering, among many other organizations, are committed to the development of new musicals. Many theatres develop both musicals and plays. New opera development is more recent trend: American Opera Company, Opera Fusion: New Works at Cincinnati Opera, and American Lyric Theatre provide valuable resources for the creation of new operas.

Traditionally, musicals premiered outside of New York before moving to Broadway. A new musical would open in New Haven or Philadelphia; during this out-of-town tryout, songs were added and eliminated. The book was revised, sometimes extensively. Changes in the creative team were not uncommon. The model has been adapted; currently, many musicals premiere at regional, nonprofit theatres with Broadway as the identified or potential target.

Often, these musicals receive Industry Readings or Workshops before their regional premieres.

Certain organizations that provide opportunities for production require staging, sets, and costumes, while others prohibit these enhancements. Some stipulate "selections" from the work, with a strict time limit. Producers should make the rules clear in their submission notices and differentiate between preferences and policies. Directors should be fully aware of any institution's procedures before rehearsals begin.

Musicals want staging. Musical theatre actors think in terms of physicality. They're trained in dancing and singing, which are presentational forms. But some unions that present readings of new musicals prohibit staging. That's the challenge of directing a reading of a new musical.

Daniella Topol, Director

The development of a musical or opera is more complex than the development of most plays. Because musicals and operas consist of multiple elements, the creative team often starts as simply as possible.

> *I like to begin the process with a creative work session that does not involve actors. We want the composer, lyricist, librettist, director and artistic director in the room together, so everyone can hear each other's ideas.*
> Cara Reichel, Producing Artistic Director,
> Prospect Theater Company

Libretto Readings

Rehearsing a musical or opera generally requires more time than a Play Reading, but various types of musical and opera Readings can be presented with limited rehearsals. These first Readings are mostly In-house.

In its early stages of development, the libretto of a new musical or opera can be examined with actors but without music. This type of isolated investigation is a useful dramaturgical step that can serve the work without the time and resources that incorporating the score demand. The creative team can examine structure, characters, relationships, tone, and style.

Recorded Score

A possible next step is a Reading that includes the score in some form. Composers can perform the songs or record them in advance with a few singers. Because actors are not asked to learn the score, this type of Reading can be rehearsed in a few days or a week. Incorporating music allows the artistic team to consider the weight and balance of the songs, alternative styles and tempos, and how the text and music work together to tell the story. The collaborators can hear the entire piece and adapt and adjust the score and libretto so they cohere into a unified whole.

Libretto Readings or Readings in which the score is incorporated but not sung by the actors are helpful for the creative team, but they are not suited for public presentation.

Piano/Vocal Workshops

Before a musical or opera is presented to the public, the score should be rehearsed by actors. The easiest way to incorporate music into the presentation with limited rehearsal is to simplify the accompaniment, using only a piano or keyboard, and to reduce or eliminate the chorus.

The amount of rehearsal needed for a piano/vocal workshop of a new musical or opera is informed by the length and complexity of the score. Staggering the rehearsals for the principal singers is an effective way to make use of time. The accompanist or conductor is the only person required at the music rehearsals, although in many cases, the composer, librettist, and director may also attend.

Depending on the orchestral requirements, the accompaniment can be augmented by an additional instrument such as piano, cello, or percussion. During the rehearsal, the composer and librettist can refine the work. With operas, which are often cast years in advance, the artistic team may have the advantage of working with the singers who will appear in the premiere production. Sections of the score can be rewritten to utilize the singers' abilities.

Workshops

Adding a chorus and orchestra, even in reduced numbers, requires additional rehearsals. But these elements play an important part in many musicals and operas, and a Reading or Workshop that includes at least a small orchestra and chorus is a necessary step in the later stages of development.

These Workshops may involve staging and choreography. Changes and revisions will occur throughout the process, and many Workshops culminate in In-house or public Readings. By the time a project is at this point of development, the "process versus product" consideration is clearly at play.

Opera Workshops

New operas are not workshopped as often as they should be, but development labs for operas are increasing. More attention is now given to using them, so things are getting better. Some companies do it very well. Workshops for operas are generally easier at smaller organizations, where there are fewer union restrictions. And the workshop can definitely determine whether or not the opera will be produced.

I prefer workshops well in advance of the premiere production— working with the composer and librettist on character and plot. With opera, unlike a play, it's expensive to change anything in rehearsal. Sometimes, the premiere cast is available. It's great when you have the actual cast. The composer can find what works best for their voices. It's best when the composer and librettist are open-minded, and eager to make changes.

Workshops are most effective when composers, librettists, singers, conductors and directors are fully prepared. Unless the producers have authorized a selection of the work, the opera should be complete so that it can be fully and accurately assessed. With so many moving parts, everything needs to be in place, at least preliminarily, for the presentation. Singers work with coaches before rehearsal, and come in knowing the material. The conductor arrives the first day and works with singers, and the director arrives later. Skilled singers who come in knowing their material increase their chances of being hired.

Kevin Newbury, Director

Casting a Reading of a Musical or Opera

Just as some actors are more effective than others at working within the bound-
aries of Play Readings, certain singers and actors are better suited for the developmental stages of new musicals or operas. Singers with a strong sense of
musicianship can use the time effectively, whereas actors who learn music by
ear generally require more rehearsal. Readings and Workshops of musicals and
operas need performers who can sight-read music, as they will likely be asked to
adjust to changes and learn new material quickly.

Materials

While musicals in which the songs and the book are separate elements are still
being written, many contemporary musicals are through-sung or consist of complex musical sequences with dialogue intertwined. The actors in Readings or
Workshops of these types of musicals require various materials to take full advantage of the rehearsal time.

The composer is usually responsible for preparing the music for rehearsal,
although when resources allow, music assistants, copyists, and others can be of great
help. Composers, librettists or stage managers must be sure that any changes made
in the score or libretto during rehearsal are reflected in all the distributed materials
so that they remain identical throughout the rehearsal process. When the materials are prepared in advance, rehearsal time can be used more purposefully.

Required Materials

- A struck-through Reading draft of the libretto with the preliminary
  edits and the lyrics to the songs in capital letters
- A full list of the songs and links to music "demos" of each
- An integrated score, which incorporates all dialogue located within
  songs in its proper place.

The Reading draft of the libretto and the integrated score should be three-
hole punched, and binders should be provided. The entire integrated score is not
distributed to everyone, as actors prepare their "books" in different ways. Some
learn the songs and use the libretto for the Reading. Others may prefer to take
pages that include their songs out of the integrated score and interpolate these
into the libretto to create a single document. Without an integrated score, actors
spend rehearsal time writing internal dialogue into the score.

The selection from the song "Rosemary" from the musical "The Flood" is an
example of an integrated score (see Diagram 13.1 and Appendix G). Notice that
the dialogue between Wright, Curtis, and Alice is written internally in the song,
where it would be spoken over the music, which is choral and does not contain
lyrics. When the dialogue is integrated into the score, the actors and singers are
not required to shift back and forth between the score and the Reading draft or
take time to write the dialogue into their scores.

WRIGHT: I'm not leaving my land. CURTIS: You can't stay here. WRIGHT: We'll be fine. Now leave us alone. ALICE: Dad!

CURTIS: C'mon, Zeke. Think of your girls.   WRIGHT: I said go!   ALICE: Dad, Rosemary-

WRIGHT: Alice, take your sister and head up to the attic.
ALICE: That's what I'm trying to tell you. Rosemary's gone!

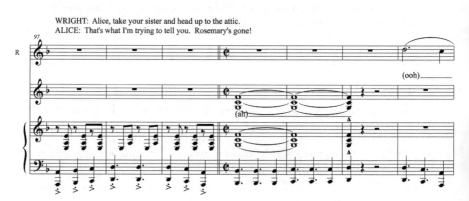

Diagram 13.1a

ROSEMARY runs on. From offstage we hear WRIGHT and ALICE calling for Rosemary.

ROSEMARY trips and falls into one of the ditches WRIGHT dug, hitting her head.

For the first time, the RIVER emerges from behind the levee
and comes forward to ROSEMARY.

Diagram 13.1b

Internal Stage Directions

As many stage directions as possible should be eliminated for a Reading or Workshop of a musical or opera. Stage directions within a song, particularly in through-sung musicals or musicals with extended song sequences, pose challenges for Readings. In many of these musicals, events occur within the song. Some of this action may be communicated physically by the actors, but certain stage directions need to be spoken. Adding a few bars of music to accommodate a spoken stage direction is possible, but this should be done sparingly, with the full approval of the composer, and only if it does not impact the flow of the song. Revising and trimming stage directions so that they fit precisely within a specific musical phrase is often necessary.

Relocating stage directions by placing them before or after the song is another option, when dramatically appropriate. But often, the action described should occur exactly where it is located or as close as possible to that moment. If the action takes place while a lyric is sung, the stage direction should be eliminated, relocated, or conveyed by the actor whenever possible. Attempting to hear a spoken stage direction while simultaneously trying to listen to a lyric can be distracting for audiences.

When the only solution is for a stage direction to be read while a character is singing, the creative team needs to determine the best placement. Sections of the song that contain held notes, vamps, wordless vocalizing, or dance music are good choices. These allow for the information to be communicated without fighting the lyrics. Directors, composers, lyricists, and librettists often work together in advance of rehearsal to make these decisions.

> *With musicals, you have to find the best place to read stage directions. A lot of times, transitional music will already be written for where the stage direction would be read, as in "the scenery flies out and she is alone." Sometimes I ask the composer or Musical Director to add music if the stage direction is integral and there isn't enough music to cover it. As a director, I prefer to edit my own stage directions, and often, I ask the writer's permission to adapt them or relocate them, as there's usually not a lot of time for back and forth. Also, I often cut unnecessary music for a reading—long intros, or anytime the actor is left standing there with nothing to act that forwards the story. Sometimes you can make use of the "extra" music for simple staging, but there must be an emotional beat that needs to be filled. Often these cuts end up in the full production.*
>
> Nick Corley, Director; Actor

With these concerns in mind, consider the selection from the integrated score of "The Flood." The stage direction *"ROSEMARY runs on. From offstage we hear WRIGHT and ALICE calling for Rosemary"* can easily be cut. The actor playing Rosemary could enter hurriedly, and the actors portraying Wright and Alice call to her from retreat positions. The stage direction *"ROSEMARY trips and falls into one of the ditches WRIGHT dug, hitting her head"* can be spoken over the held notes, where the chorus is singing wordlessly. If the stage direction takes longer to read than the held notes, it should be shortened. As always, a care-ful examination of the script will determine the most effective cuts. If trimming is required, the artistic team should decide whether it is more important for the audience to hear *"WRIGHT dug"* or *"hitting her head."*

Further down on the same page is the stage direction *"For the first time, the RIVER emerges from behind the levee and comes forward to ROSEMARY"* (The RIVER is a character in "The Flood"). The stage direction could be cut, and the action conveyed by the actor. If it needs to be read, this could happen over the vamp at the bottom of the page.

While various solutions exist for all of the demands, extensive pre-rehearsal preparation for musicals and operas is important.

CHAPTER 14

NONDEVELOPMENTAL READINGS

The primary focus of this book is Play Readings in the context of new play development. However, many theatres, schools, libraries, museums, publishing houses, literary clubs, historical societies, and other organizations present Readings of classic or previously produced plays and musicals or selections from historical documents, texts, and speeches. The uses of these Nondevelopmental Readings are vast and varied.

Plays

Many theatres that devote their programming to classics present Readings of obscure texts. These Readings expose audiences to unfamiliar works and may inform programming. They are open to the general public and can be benefits, galas, or fundraisers. Red Bull Theater, Mint Theater Company, Shakespeare's Globe, and Project Shaw are among the many companies that present such Readings.

Little-known plays by recognized or neglected playwrights are increasingly presented as part of a commitment by these theatres to bring worthy work to light. Like new plays, they offer outstanding roles for actors and a chance to create characters without reference or prototype. These Play Readings expose theatregoers to a canon of unknown texts that will likely never receive full productions.

> With Red Bull Theater's Revelation Readings, we've developed a following for rarely produced plays. We use them as an exploration for possible programming, and some readings have gone on to full productions. Readings can change my mind about what we produce. But they are a value in and of themselves. Many of the classic plays we do were written for the ear more than the eye, with beautiful, resonant language. They are a great way to expand the nature of our programming.
>
> Jesse Berger, Artistic Director, Red Bull Theater

Nondevelopmental Readings also give audiences an increasingly rare opportunity to see plays with large casts. Contemporary playwrights are well aware that large-cast plays have fewer chances of production. Prior to the twenty-first century, playwrights rarely considered cast size: Plays were often written with roles for as many as fifty actors. A full production of a large-cast play today would be cost-prohibitive for many theatres. Considerable doubling would be necessary, or characters would need to be eliminated. Readings of large-cast plays allow audiences to experience these works in their original scope and grandeur. That said, even Readings of these plays often reduce the number of actors by doubling many small roles.

Musicals

Despite the increasing number of Nondevelopmental Readings of straight plays, musicals dominate the nondevelopmental landscape. The rich catalogue of neglected twentieth century musicals is now presented in a variety of Reading formats. The spectrum ranges from the Play Reading model with actors at music stands and piano accompaniment to presentations that suggest full productions with staging, choreography, sets, costumes, and orchestras.

Encores!, Great American Musicals in Concert, and The York Theatre Company's Musicals in Mufti series present underappreciated shows written by many of this country's most heralded composers, lyricists, and librettists. Some are offered as originally written or with minor changes. In many cases, the material is substantially revised. The term "revisal" is currently used to describe a significantly reworked presentation of previously produced material.

Many of the more fully conceived presentations are partially memorized. Others are completely memorized, with staging and choreography. While they lay outside the scope of this book, the form grew directly out of Readings and Workshops, which have informed how new musicals are presented. These musicals are a curious hybrid: They offer more production elements than a Reading but are not as elaborately produced as most Broadway shows, although some have transferred to Broadway.

As with Readings of pre-twenty-first-century plays, the most cited reason for presenting Readings of obscure musicals is that they would be cost-prohibitive to produce in full productions. Moreover, despite the many virtues of these shows, which often feature outstanding scores and orchestrations, the librettos can be problematic, which is why they are frequently edited and adapted.

Readings of neglected musicals give contemporary audiences a chance to hear scores performed live, which are remembered mostly through the original cast albums. And where an orchestra is utilized, audiences can experience the original arrangements in their full glory. These presentations are a gift to musical theatre aficionados.

Many Readings of musicals are also presented simply, with minimal staging and a few production elements. This "bare-bones" approach can allow an audience to experience the material more purely, without the encumbrances of a large production musicals often employ. In some cases, the original composers and lyricists revisit the material and refine it for the Reading.

Some classic musicals failed because the original productions were overblown and the shows were dragged down by them. Sometimes, too much is spelled out in the physical production, and this can work against the material. It depends on the show, but in many cases, simpler is better. In a reading, the material can come through more clearly, and the audience's imagination is put into play.

We don't rewrite the shows we do in Musicals in Mufti. We may make a few edits based on the need for a smaller cast size, but it's our mission to stick as closely as possible to what the show was, or hoped to be. Sometimes, we will revise a show based on the writers' notes from the estate. Or if the writers are around and want to retool it, we love that. That has happened with all sorts of people, from Comden & Green, to Jones & Schmidt, to Cryer & Ford, and Bock & Harnick. And others.

James Morgan, Producing Artistic Director,
York Theatre Company

Other Venues

Increasingly, colleges, universities, and even high schools present Readings of classic or published plays to expose students to the history of dramatic literature. These performances are an introduction to the world of Play Readings for many student audiences—as well as emerging writers, directors, and actors, and may be used to inform programming.

We do readings of classical and contemporary plays at Lewis-Clark State College to acquaint the audiences with unfamiliar work. You can get a sense of the story from just hearing a play, by focusing on the language and listening. You realize the importance of language and images in a way that might be harder to do in a full production.

Nancy Lee-Painter, Associate Professor of
Theatre, Lewis-Clark Stage College

Libraries, museums, and historical societies also program Readings of published plays, documents, speeches, and selections from transcripts and nonfiction works. They are often presented simply, at music stands, though period costumes may be used. These theatrical presentations are valuable additions to libraries' or museums' exhibits.

At the Abraham Lincoln Presidential Library and Museum, we do readings of selections from biographies or historical documents. Usually, they are forty-five minutes pieces. The performances take place during museum hours, and the show is an extra program for museum visitors. The staging is very simple, and we look for actors who can best honor the texts. Elegant prose lends itself well to a reading. Recently, we presented a Performance Reading from "Team of Rivals" by Doris Kearns Goodwin, a brilliant biography of Lincoln. She granted permission, attended the first performance, and was very pleased. We used ten actors as multiple narrators, and one actor portrayed Lincoln. I don't see what we do as plays. They are programs. But it's civilized, in this day and age, to hear the written word aloud.

Phil Funkenbusch, Director, Shows Division,
Abraham Lincoln Presidential Library and Museum

Considerations with Nondevelopmental Readings

Most of the same guidelines apply to presenting a Nondevelopmental Reading of a play or musical as apply to a Reading of a new work. Producers should be clear with the artistic team about the purpose of the Reading—most importantly, whether the presentation is a "one-off" or whether it is being considered for production or transfer. The artistic team should also be informed of any policies or preferences regarding the Reading itself; do the producers want a standard Reading or a fully staged presentation?

With works that are in the public domain, directors have the right to edit and adapt the material. However, the occasion to hear a neglected play or musical can be compromised if the work is extensively altered. While the presentation of works that are not in the public domain can benefit if stage directions are edited, the producer must obtain permission from the publisher or the writer to do so.

AFTER THE READING

CHAPTER 15

AUDIENCES AND TALKBACKS

Many theatres have built devoted audiences for Play Readings who appreciate hearing new work. Merely attending a Reading provides audiences with a chance to participate indirectly in the development process.

Audience Reaction

In performance, an audience's reaction is critical to helping me understand whether the work is succeeding. It is almost impossible for the audience not to be truthful about their emotional and intellectual engagement. If they are focused on the stage then they are involved. It is a much more important test than whether they say they like or dislike it.
David Esbjornsen, Director

Theatres and playwrights should give audiences a chance to interact with new work. It's through this interaction that play-goers become invested in the programming process, and share in that. Theatres can educate audiences about the process of play development, and what's more, have a duty to educate their audiences about the process of crafting a play.
Amy Rose Marsh, Literary Manager,
Samuel French, Inc.

The people who come to see readings are not always the people who come to see shows. This happens more often than I thought. I love a super-invested, respectful audience.
Caridad Svich, Playwright

Playwrights should listen to the audience response and reaction during a reading, so they can hear where there is confusion or resistance. Where audience members are often wrong, audiences in the aggregate are always right.
Ralph Sevush, Esq., Executive Director/Business and Legal
Affairs, Dramatists Guild of America, Inc.

Talkbacks provide more direct involvement. They allow general audiences to respond to the artists and to offer their opinions. Talkbacks can also enlighten audiences and teach them to sharpen their critical skills. These audiences play a vital part in the current model of new play development and deserve respect for their support of new work.

General audiences enjoy meeting creative artists. They are intrigued to hear playwrights discuss the work, and are impressed by what the director and actors can accomplish with so little time. Most audience members are courteous and generous-spirited.

> *Just a simple note to say thank you to Queens Theatre for the opportunity and the thrill of viewing the selection of new play readings each season. For my wife and I to be able to talk to the cast and have words with the playwright at the end of each event, to discuss the play and storyline, to give our opinion, it is wonderful and exciting for us both. Please continue this special program!*
>
> Sy and Rochelle Wichel, Audience Members

Some playwrights enjoy talkbacks and public responses. They learn from insightful observations, ignore irrelevant comments, and are impervious to inappropriate remarks. Other writers are extremely vulnerable following a Reading and find a public forum for discussion of their work uncomfortable and even frightening.

Every institution has the right to decide if a Reading will be followed by a post-show discussion.

A producer should let a playwright know when accepting the offer for a Reading whether it will be followed by a talkback and whether the playwright and the actors will be required to take part. Ideally, when organizations include talkbacks as part of their programming, playwrights and actors should have the choice of whether or not to participate. However, even when they are not required, many feel obligated.

Playwrights who are opposed to talkbacks should not submit their work to theatres that require them to be involved. If playwrights are averse to public remarks from respondents at a festival, they should consider whether to submit their work to such an organization.

Arguments against Talkbacks

Certain people who attend Readings—both theatre insiders and general audiences—enjoy expounding their views in talkbacks. They are persuaded that they know exactly how every play can be improved. Some seem to relish the chance to be critical, and are occasionally cruel. Invariably, obtuse comments will be offered as sage advice. The remarks can sting. Because of unpleasant experiences with so-called talkbacks, certain theatre artists have come to see the audience as rivals.

Talking Back to Talkbacks

Talkbacks are like brain surgery. If the audience is bored in Act Two, the problem may be in Act One. Audiences wouldn't know that. Playwrights know the most about this process. Everyone else is there to support them. Playwrights shouldn't be at the bottom rung.

Anne Cattaneo, Dramaturg, Lincoln Center Theater

Talkbacks are useless. Giving feedback is a learned skill, and audiences don't have it. Playwrights shouldn't be expected to heed specific suggestions from the audience.

Ralph Sevush, Esq., Executive Director/Business and Legal Affairs, Dramatists Guild of America, Inc.

Talkbacks are useful but in my opinion, they are mostly for public relations. In certain instances audience feedback can be helpful but you need to carefully sort through the individual comments. Only a small percentage of the remarks will enlighten the playwright and director. Mostly, it tends to give them bouts of anxiety. Often, the audience is more interested in what they might want the play to be rather than what the playwright is attempting. They often target a part of the play that they are convinced is failing when in fact it might be the most important idea in the script and simply hasn't found its clarity or full expression yet. Producers and literary managers should guide the playwrights and their companies through these experiences. Those who open up a production to the audience have a responsibility to protect the artists.

David Esbjornsen, Director

Terminologies and Alternatives

The term "talkback" is unfortunate in the context of new play development. The word itself implies confrontation. Children talk back to their parents. Students talk back to teachers. Adults talk back to authority figures. Everyone talks back to the television. And following many Readings, audiences talk back to playwrights.

There is no nonconfrontational application for the term "talkback" outside of new play development. Its use may encourage audiences to address playwrights confrontationally. As for "feedback," the term smacks of regurgitation. As Maria Callas remarks in Terrence McNally's "Master Class," "What an ugly word!"

If a theatre, lab, or producing organization chooses to solicit input from the audience following a public presentation, "discussion," "conversation," or "Q & A" are more suitable terms. Revising the nomenclature will not eliminate the risks involved when audiences are invited to share their thoughts, but it is a step in the right direction.

There are valid alternatives to post-show conversations. Questionnaires inserted in the printed programs have many advantages: They remove the potentially provoking quality of talkbacks, they give the audience a chance to consider the play in private, and they eliminate the risk of persuasion by consensus. Also, playwrights have the choice of whether or not to read them.

> *I'm not a fan of the word "talkback." The Lark doesn't do talkbacks, but rather has the audience respond in a written format. There are a few specific questions everyone is asked to respond to and then these responses are typed up and can be retrieved by the playwright whenever they'd like—be it the following week, month or year.*
>
> Lisa Rothe, Director; Director of Global Exchange,
> Lark Playwrights Center

Moderators

Because talkbacks can be fraught with peril, there is a near consensus that any Q&A or conversation following a Reading should be moderated. All post-performance discussions need someone to facilitate. Playwrights should not be required to moderate a talkback. It is important that the conversation focuses on the play itself, and not the Reading. A skilled moderator can pose questions and guide the discussion. They can discourage the audience from offering suggestions or solutions, as well as tactfully solve any problem that arises. Experts on issues raised by the play can also be invited to participate in the discussion.

If an audience member attempts to dominate the discussion, the moderator can say something as simple as "We'd like to hear from as many people as possible." If a harsh judgment is offered, the moderator can ask the audience, "How many agree with that observation?" Most audience members are as frustrated with tactless remarks as playwrights. Moderators have the power to control the tone and content of the event.

The moderator should tell the audience the length of the discussion when it begins. The creative team has likely been rehearsing all day, and a fifteen-minute discussion is usually enough time for a Q&A. After fifteen minutes, the moderator can say, "We have time for one more question."

Facilitating the Discussion

Talkbacks can be brutal, cruel, unhelpful, and even harmful. Or they can be transformative for the artists and for the audience. A moderator is critical in that dynamic.

Laura Penn, Executive Director, Society of Stage
Directors and Choreographers

I love curated talkbacks, with specific questions. What moments engaged you? What will you remember? Did any character get lost for you? The audience really becomes a part of the process, listening to each other talk, and piggy-backing off of each other.
> Susan Louise O'Connor, Actor

If there is going to be a conversation afterward, someone has to facilitate the discussion. There are various effective models. Asking an audience what images or text popped out for them, or what they will still be thinking about a few weeks from now, can be useful information for the playwright. I know New York Theatre Workshop effectively uses the Liz Lerman Critical Response Process as a tool for responding to work. In these discussions, it's important that the playwright feels safe and there is a sense of community. Playwrights should never have to be put on the defensive.
> Lisa Rothe, Director; Director of Global Exchange,
> Lark Playwrights Center

At the discussion following the reading, we don't encourage the playwrights to talk, or the audience to talk directly to the playwrights. This is to protect the writer. The moderator asks the audience what they enjoyed about the play, where their mind may have wandered during the reading as well as any specific questions the playwright wants the audience to address, which are solicited in advance, and asked by the moderator. Playwrights shouldn't feel the need to explain their play, or be required to. They've done their work. It's in the play or it's not.
> Kim T. Sharp, Literary Manager,
> Abingdon Theatre Company

Playwrights' Choice

It is not inevitable that a talkback follows a Play Reading. Certain theatres discourage or prohibit them. Other institutions have specific policies for how the discussions are run. Doing away with talkbacks or stipulating alternative approaches presuppose that playwrights must be protected from the audience. For certain writers, this is inarguably the case, but it is not true for all.

Playwrights should have a say in how post-show discussions are handled. Often, they have specific questions they would like to ask the audience, such as "Were you able to track all of the off-stage characters?" "We eliminated references to dates in the stage directions—could you follow the passage of time between scenes?" They can discover if an aspect of the play that seemed obvious to them is unclear to the audience. If an audience member is confused by something in the play, the writer should hear it as an observation, not an absolute.

Some writers actually benefit from audience members' remarks. While most general audiences lack the skills to assess the work dramaturgically, their comments can offer "civilian" perspectives, distinct from those of industry insiders who populate the audience at many Readings. Their observations can be particularly helpful with mainstream plays.

That said, many playwrights' questions are answered best by sitting among the audience and assessing their reactions during the Reading. And most playwrights prefer discussing the work with their friends and collaborators rather than with a room full of strangers.

Playwrights Talk Back

When I've been living with the play for a long time, the audience response at a reading can tell me about the experience of the play—if they were surprised when I wanted them to be surprised and so on. But I have mixed feelings about talkbacks. If there's going to be a talkback, it's good to know the specific purpose and goal. Generally, it's more helpful for me to talk to friends I trust who might know the play and my writing better. For me, it all depends on where I am in the process.

Lauren Yee, Playwright

I appreciate when an audience at a talkback is curious about the inspiration for the play. Sometimes, this makes me revisit my original intention. But audience suggestions are never helpful. I've already considered all those choices.

Don Nguyen, Playwright

I have found talkbacks useful for a play in its earlier stages when the people "talking back" are friends and trusted theater professionals. I have found audience talkbacks useful when a play is in previews, but not before.

Rajiv Joseph, Playwright

Not every play needs a talkback. It depends on the play, and if the subject matter asks for conversation. It can be damaging. You're processing a lot already. And writers always remember the remarks that make no sense. Sometimes the audience wants to be "on stage," and they use the talkback for that. If talkbacks are short, they're better. And writers should decide if they want one. Talkbacks can go into "Facebook" mode—like me/don't like me. I prefer if audience members chat with me privately after. What's more useful is discussing the play with the artistic team. That's like an architect getting together with the builders.

Caridad Svich, Playwright

Discussions with the audience and remarks from respondents after a Reading compel playwrights to hone their skills at sifting through notes to determine which are useful and which are not. All theatre artists must weigh contradictory comments on their work—not only from audiences but also from friends, colleagues, collaborators, producers, and critics.

Notes

Playwrights should hear all suggestions, but that doesn't mean they should take all suggestions.
> Ralph Sevush, Esq. Executive Director/Business and Legal
> Affairs, Dramatists Guild of America, Inc.

As an educator, I find talkback, feedback and respondents' comments useful for playwrights. If they don't understand something in the play, they can communicate what was communicated to them. This helps playwrights learn how to hear and interpret notes.
> Julie Mollenkamp, KCACTF National Playwriting
> Program Chair, Region 5

I would recommend, when receiving notes from anyone, to know in your heart which notes are interesting, and which notes are terrible. Consider the interesting ones, and don't take the terrible ones.
> Rajiv Joseph, Playwright

CHAPTER 16

FOLLOW-UP DISCUSSIONS

Playwrights

Following a Reading, a representative of the producing organization will usually thank the creative team for their work, in person or by email. The artists should respond in kind. Almost every Reading is a learning experience, and all theatre artists should be thankful to any organization that offered its resources.

Playwrights are also entitled to a follow-up discussion with a representative of any institution that presents a Reading of their work. At many festivals, the remarks by respondents or adjudicators following the Reading constitute the follow-up discussion. At most labs, conversations with the playwright following a Reading are an expected part of the process.

But while some theatres inform the playwright with the initial offer that a discussion will take place at some point following the Reading, at many theatres, no specific procedure is in place.

> *Whether there is a follow-up conversation with the playwright following the reading varies, depending on the degree of interest in the play. It's appropriate for playwrights to seek input, and helpful if they are open to ideas. Hopefully, the playwright knows what to work on. We may request a new draft, but the decision is up to the playwright.*
>
> Kim T. Sharp, Literary Manager,
> Abingdon Theatre Company

New plays serve various needs for theatres. A Reading series may generate funding and increase audience support. These are valid reasons to present Readings, but playwrights who hear nothing from producing organizations following a Reading can feel that their work has been used as "product."

> *Theatre is an industry where there can be lots of discounting of the writers. The gatekeepers won't talk to you. If you're a bank, they talk to you. It's the climate of ferocious gatekeeping that creates such a harsh climate for playwrights. The company*

stops talking to you. You don't feel like you're part of the conver-
sation. It feels like work-for-hire.

Caridad Svich, Playwright

As soon as possible after the Reading, a representative from the organization should contact the playwright to set a time to talk in person or by phone.
If playwrights do not hear from the theatre promptly, they should be patient.
Producers are usually involved with multiple projects. They may need to gather
their thoughts, to discuss the play with the literary staff, to wait until the Reading
series is complete, or to find time in their schedules.

But playwrights should not be left in the dark. A prolonged delay between the
Reading and contact from a producer puts writers in limbo; they anxiously await
any word and assume the worst. What should playwrights do in such cases?

If a writer does not hear from a producing organization after a reasonable
period of time—approximately a month—he or she should email the producer
to request a follow-up discussion. While writers may be most interested to know
if there is interest in further development or production, it helps if they have a
genuine desire to hear the producer's thoughts. If the playwright does not hear
back in a few weeks, a second email is in order.

In the follow-up discussion, playwrights should be receptive to any observations. While they need not agree, they should consider all input without resistance. Insightful perceptions and pertinent questions are appreciated by most
writers, who should also be encouraged to express their own ideas on what they
learned about the play from the Reading and what they intend to work on. Audience reaction during the Reading can be considered; however, the quality of the
Reading itself is secondary.

After a reading, I start the discussion with the playwright by ask-
ing what he or she is thinking—where they're at—and I shape
my comments to their needs. The entire discussion is framed by
what the writer says. We want them to tell the story they want
to tell, which is also the best story they could tell. I ask ques-
tions, and I listen. There may be discrepancies between what's in
the writer's head and what's on the page. I try to offer feedback
about what's best for the play, but I never give prescriptive notes
or request a specific rewrite.

Elizabeth Frankel, Literary Manager,
The Public Theater

Playwrights should be aware that while producers, artistic directors, and literary managers are in a position of power regarding the future of the work at
that organization, these individuals are offering opinions. Their remarks reveal
a personal reaction and perhaps the view of the theatre. Audiences at talkbacks
receive the bulk of the blame for irrelevant or inappropriate comments, but no
one is immune, even theatre professionals.

Producers should be as candid as possible about any future for the piece and
the writer at that organization. If they pass, they may offer to present a Reading

of another play by the writer or offer a commission. They may recommend opportunities unconnected with their theatre.

> *We are very honest with the writers about the chances of production up front. And if we don't select the play, we may invite the writer to submit another play, or act as advocate for the play at other theatres.*
>
> Nick Connaughton, Creative Entertainment
> Manager, Arcola Theatre

In the best-case scenario, the producer will contact the playwright and say, "We will produce your play." Although this happens less frequently than playwrights hope, it is possible. Playwrights also like to hear "We may produce your play." Other than these responses, most playwrights prefer to hear "We will not be producing your play" than to hear nothing at all.

Often, when producers fail to contact playwrights following a Reading or respond in vague terms, they do so out of courtesy. They are trying to protect writers. They assume that hearing "We won't be producing your play" will be devastating. But while playwrights rarely want to hear that a theatre is passing on their play, at least it is a definite response.

If a representative from the theatre requests rewrites, the purpose of the rewrites should be clearly identified; is the producer willing to read another draft when the rewrites are complete? Whenever possible, playwrights should know whether a possibility for production is contingent on the suggested rewrites, particularly those with which the writer may disagree. When a theatre is considering the play for production, writers must carefully weigh whether or not to implement suggestions that they question or dispute. Offers for production contingent on rewrites create delicate situations that producers and playwrights must handle carefully, with full transparency.

When they feel strongly, playwrights should hold their ground. If they are too open to revision and agree to make changes they do not fully support, they may waste their time and weaken their play. In many cases, producers who have a genuine interest in the play will defer to the writers' judgments.

If the producing organization does not contact the playwright after a Reading and fails to respond to the writer's requests for a follow-up discussion, they have very likely passed. This does not justify their lack of response, but if a theatre is interested in a play, they will let the writer know. Playwrights should expect at least a "rejection email" from any organization to which they have submitted their work and from any organization that presents their work.

Despite the popular idiom "No news is good news," when a theatre does not follow up with a playwright or respond to a request to discuss the play, the tacit understanding is that "No news is bad news." Contemporary playwrights, unfortunately, have become accustomed to this.

Rejection assumed by nonresponse is unfair to writers. Despite limited resources, busy schedules, changes in staff that shift programming policies, or delays caused by waiting for funding or grants, any theatre, lab, or producing organization that presents a Reading should make time for a follow-up discussion, however brief, with the playwright. This is common courtesy and common sense.

However, a production is not contingent on one theatre's interest. Other opportunities exist. Playwrights should learn what they can from the Reading, continue to work on the play, submit it elsewhere, write new plays, and move on.

Directors

Directing a Reading provides an occasion to explore a collaborative relationship. If the Reading is a success, hitting the bull's-eye is always a possibility; the theatre will produce the play, and the playwright and the theatre want the director to move forward with the project.

But even if the Reading goes well and the theatre decides to produce or to continue to develop the play, directors have no guarantee that they will remain involved. That is a harsh reality for directors who have worked diligently on the play before the Reading and during rehearsals and who genuinely admire the material. The reality is compounded when a director has been involved with numerous Readings of the same play and made valuable dramaturgical contributions.

The playwright may want to continue the collaboration, but in many cases, they do not have final say. For Readings, playwrights often choose the director, but with Workshops and full productions, producers have significantly more say. Level of success becomes as important as talent. At many theatres, emerging or midcareer directors are replaced by directors who have worked on Broadway or at the major nonprofit theatres.

> *In the rehearsal room, the director is in complete control, charged with keeping it all together. Outside the room, directors have no real authority. They don't schedule, hire or fire, write checks, or have any budget authority. They are viewed by some colleagues as being well taken care of, when in fact, they're neither fish nor fowl. They're in power, but have no power.*
> Laura Penn, Executive Director, Society of Stage Directors and Choreographers

The current model of new play development does not protect directors who shepherd a play through various Readings. Many directors devote considerable time and energy to the material only to be removed if the play moves on to a full production or if a different theatre expresses interest. The director and playwright can generate a contract that stipulates that the director is "attached" to the play for a certain period of time. This contract can also include "right of first refusal," which offers remuneration to directors if they are replaced. But contracts are rare for Play Readings, and producing organizations discourage this type of encumbrance.

Directors should seek to develop relationships with playwrights whose work they admire and who will recommend them. Playwrights need directors who understand their work and have the skill and vision to bring it to life on stage. They both want a trusted collaborator. Playwrights who have developed productive relationships with directors often want them involved from the earliest stages of a play's development. When the director and playwright are previous or frequent collaborators, producers most often honor the relationship.

To gain the support and trust of playwrights, directors must perform effectively at every stage of the process, beginning with the discussions before the Reading. Playwrights appreciate directors who organize a Reading effectively, who speak about the play intelligently, who use their time purposefully, and who shape the actors' performances convincingly.

If a director enjoyed working on the Reading and admires the play, he or she should contact the playwright and arrange a time to talk. The discussion should be open and collegial, not an attempt to solidify an attachment to the play. The director should not offer critical remarks or suggestions about the play unless the writer requests them. However, directors should give a frank assessment of their own work on the Reading. Directors can let writers know that they would be interesting in reading their new plays.

Directors who do not feel strongly about the play should not attempt to meet. Playwrights need directors who are enthusiastic about their work. And for whatever reasons, if the playwright is not interested in pursuing further collaboration, he or she should let the director know as gently as possible. Directors also need appreciative collaborators. There are many plays and many playwrights. Directors can seek out other opportunities.

Actors

An actor's attachment to a play following a Reading is often more tenuous than a director's. The best reasons for actors to be involved in Readings are to support the playwright, to make contacts, and to assist in creating new work. Any expectations beyond those should not be rationale for participation.

Following a Reading, actors can email the producer, director, playwright, and fellow actors to let them know that they appreciated the opportunity. These emails are best when they include specifics. Playwrights want to hear what actors value about their work. Directors like to know that they helped guide an actor's performance. Producers appreciate when actors tell them that the Reading was well organized, that the artistic team was treated courteously by the staff, and that the sandwiches were delicious. If for any reason the Reading was unsatisfying, the actor can email a simple "thank you" when it is over and leave it at that. However, most Readings are worthwhile experiences for actors.

Many actors who participate in Readings find great satisfaction in helping playwrights learn about their plays. Jumping into a creative process can be invigorating. While not a substitute for production, participating in a Reading is part of what it means to be a contemporary actor. The model of new play development in contemporary theatre relies on their talent and altruism.

Emails and Social Media

One of the rewards of Play Readings is that they bring together groups of theatre artists and prospective collaborators. When the rehearsal process is rewarding and the Reading is a success, the artistic team can take pride in the accomplishment. Some of the creative team may want to stay in touch.

Given that emails have likely been sent to the entire team, unless the emails were "blind carbon copied (Bcc)," everyone involved in the Reading will have contact information for all of the participants. Apart from a thank-you email, which can be Cc'd (carbon copied), if the artists involved with the Reading are to be added to any eblast list, they should be Bcc'd. A Cc allows recipients to see everyone's email address. Most recipients do not want their email addresses made public.

Following the Reading, theatre artists can notify each other about certain upcoming projects. However, they need not send eblasts about every project. Playwrights, directors, and actors should be selective and notify colleagues only about work that shows them to their best advantage. It is not necessary to add everyone involved with every Reading to an eblast list of friends and colleagues. It is best to invite specific people to specific projects.

Eblasts and social media are useful tools for theatre artists to inform producers and colleagues about upcoming projects, but they often function more as notifications than invitations. Even if they do not attend, people in the industry learn about projects and artists through these communications.

Recipients of both Bcc and Cc notifications are aware that the email has been sent to multiple recipients. In many cases, personal emails are more suitable. This can be easily done by forwarding the eblast to individual recipients with a personalized note. When a theatre artist is hopeful that a specific person will attend, a personalized email is important, but it should not be worded in a manner that suggests an obligation. And while a personal reminder is routine, repeated emails about the same project become tiresome.

When adding someone to an eblast list, theatre artists should make it easy for recipients to unsubscribe. If the eblast is generated by an email marketing company, it should include an unsubscribe option. If the eblasts are personally generated, a statement such as "Please let me know if you prefer not to receive future emails" is useful.

Online fundraising campaigns, known as crowdfunding, are more recent phenomena driven by economics. These are legitimate methods of raising money to fund a production, although donors should be aware that various policies exist as to what happens to the funds if the project is not realized. Crowdsourcing and social media are also transforming the ways in which productions are promoted. Facebook, Twitter, and Instagram can be valuable promotional tools.

The same principles apply to social media notifications, email marketing company notifications, online fundraising campaigns, and crowdsourcing platforms: Theatre artists should not send multiple notifications and should make it as easy as possible for recipients to opt out.

Most theatre insiders appreciate a notification about an upcoming project, particularly from someone whose work they respect. They do not mind the occasional solicitation for funds, but no one should be assailed with continuous notifications and solicitations. And any information that is not theatre related should be strictly avoided. Personal, political, or religious matters should be restricted to family and friends.

EPILOGUE: MOVING FORWARD

How did we arrive at the current model of new play development? When did it begin? Who were the theatre artists and companies responsible? Who were the visionaries? Traditionally, new plays premiered on Broadway. This was followed by the Off-Broadway and Off-Off-Broadway movements in the 1950s and 1960s. That rich and fascinating phase of theatre history gave way to one in which a small number of nonprofit theatres and labs became the leaders in new play development and pioneered our current model.

The transitional period from Off-Off-Broadway to the early nonprofits is underexplored and eminently worthy of study. Many of the people who created theatre during that time, some of whom I interviewed for this book, are eager to tell their stories, which would be of tremendous value to all theatre artists. As a result of their efforts, an upsurge of theatres, labs, and other organizations across the country and the world began to develop and present new work.

While variations of the current models have been in place since the 1970s, they continue to expand and evolve. The models are in need of improvement and experimentation. No attempt has been made in this book to pin down particular institutions' policies, as they are constantly in flux. This is healthy.

While some theatre artists resist the current models of development, producers, artistic directors, and literary staff are continuously exploring and devising ways in which they can assist playwrights in the creation of new work. I am astonished by the dedication and fervor of the individuals involved in steering new plays to production. While many have contradictory views, their commitment is unquestionable. We live in a heady time for new plays, rife with potential.

Some writers operate almost exclusively outside the current models of development. Some thrive within them. Most find ways of navigating through the shifting waters. While some approaches privilege playwrights and others are audience driven or profit based, theatres cannot exist without new plays to fill their stages. Different playwrights benefit from different methods, and all writers must decide what works best for them.

> *Every play is its own world, and the needs of every play and playwright are different. And they are going to change. Follow the contours of the writing newly each time.*
>
> Adam Greenfield, Associate Artistic Director,
> Playwrights Horizons

The number of theatres, labs, and other organizations that develop new work continues to grow. This results in more opportunities for playwrights. While New York City may still hold a privileged position, opportunities abound for regional productions of new plays that have never been produced in New York.

In many ways, New York theatre *is* regional theatre—the region is Manhattan. Audiences in other boroughs of New York City are different from Manhattan audiences, and theatres in Queens and Brooklyn cater to these audiences' tastes. Cities such as Chicago, Washington D.C., and Seattle, as well as smaller communities across the country, program new plays that reflect local playwrights' perspectives and local audiences' tastes.

> *What's great about American theatre is the variety of paths open to playwrights. Moving to New York City is no longer the only option. There are MFA programs and theatres across the country; you can live in Austin or D.C. or a smaller community and be incredibly successful. Some theatres certainly still use the New York Times as their literary agent, but because of organizations like the National New Play Network, there are more regionally-focused playwrights, more playwrights who live outside the major cities that are still able to connect their own experiences to other regions beyond where they live. Doing a play reading in new region can be extremely useful. The playwright is able to see how it will land with different patron communities.*
>
> Jojo Ruf, Managing Director, Laboratory for
> Global Performance and Politics, Georgetown University;
> former Executive Director, National New Play Network

New York may be the home of splashy Broadway musicals and edgy Off-Broadway voices, but many audiences crave mainstream, family-friendly fare. The current landscape provides an array of production opportunities for playwrights. There is no need for writers to apologize for a desire to create work that appeals to general audiences.

> *It's not entirely true that no one makes money as playwright; we have a surprising number of writers whose plays really do well in the amateur market, outside of the often talked about new play channels. The theatre-consuming market is vast, and there are many different audiences, including high schools and community theatres, which do their own and often different work that professional theatres. We represent all kinds of playwrights who want to make theatre happen for people. Some of them will never have plays in or around New York, but will find success in other markets.*
>
> *Working at Samuel French is about tapping into the marriage of progressive writing and commercial writing. They can coexist. Our job here is not to be "taste pirates," or tell theatres the artistic value of something. Our job is to bring art to the people, and not to judge their tastes. The reasons that theatres do plays*

are vast and various, and we love all our audiences and writers equally. And we understand that they want different things, and that every play will have its own trajectory.

Amy Rose Marsh, Literary Manager,
Samuel French, Inc.

Many theatre artists who experienced the Off-Off-Broadway scene or who were involved with the small group of nonprofit theatres that followed are justifiably nostalgic for the sense of community they enjoyed. The culture has undergone an upheaval, and artists of all disciplines struggle to create in an increasingly corporate mindset. Not only playwrights but also novelists, poets, painters, sculptors, singers, musicians, and all artists inhabit a different world than their predecessors. There is no turning back.

Artists in all fields must find or make their own communities. The growth of writers groups is one example of how playwrights have met this challenge. Writers groups are part of many theatres' new play programs. Playwrights can apply or are invited to join. These groups provide a home base for writers to share their work with peers. They function as "support groups" where writers can complain, commiserate, and encourage. While there is no direct path to production, writers groups provide something valuable: a sense of shared values and common interests. Many writers groups now exist without a host theatre, created by playwrights themselves.

I've been involved, and continue to be involved with many writers groups. In addition to dramaturgical input on a new play, it's great to just be able to talk to people who know about the process of writing. You become invested in other people's work—and inspired by it. Some of these people have become lifelong friends.

Don Nguyen, Playwright

One of the best ways for writers to avoid feeling isolated in an increasingly product-driven environment is to maintain a network of like-minded peers involved in theatre. Many of the playwrights I interviewed for this book expressed a similar sentiment: When faced with the challenges of grappling with an enormous industry or sifting through comments from artistic directors, literary staffs, and audiences, playwrights turn to friends and colleagues for advice and support.

The vast and varied methods of new play development will continue to evolve with the introduction of new technologies. Playwrights have begun to attend out-of-town auditions and rehearsals on Skype and participate in post-Reading discussions via cell phones. Ecologically minded theatres have begun to do away with programs; perhaps scripts for Readings will be eliminated entirely, replaced with tablets, allowing rewrites to be instantly implemented. Musicians have already begun to use tablets in place of scores in public performances, and significant changes have taken place in the technology of music preparation. The ways in which technology will inform new play development are immeasurable.

But despite technological advancements, playwrights will continue to spend much of their time alone. For many writers, one of the most significant advantages of Play Readings is that they put playwrights in a room where they can interact with other theatre artists. Readings allow writers to get out of their homes and away from the isolation of their electronic devices. Theatre has become collaborative sooner.

Additionally, Play Readings are often free of charge, and what with rising ticket prices, Readings can be the only way for audiences on limited budgets to experience theatre. Also, given the short rehearsal period, actors and directors who have full time "day jobs" can stay involved in theatre through Readings.

A tough reality that confronts all playwrights is that most new plays will never be produced. Producers and artistic directors insist that they want to present more new work, yet there is a surplus of theatre artists of all disciplines. And while Readings are not effective substitutes for full productions, for most playwrights, directors, and actors, they are better than no production at all.

> *Readings can be beautiful as performances. This validates readings. Who knows if the play will ever have a full production?*
> Ian Morgan, Associate Artistic Director,
> Director, New Group

It may be difficult for playwrights to understand why some of their work is not produced. But a play stuck in development may not be the writer's best work. They are entitled to feel differently, but writers and all theatre artists must learn to accept rejection.

> *You wrote a play but the producers passed. Why? There are three reasons. One: The producers are crazy. Two: They know it's good, but it's not for them. Three: It's not a good play. The only thing playwrights can control is the last one.*
> Gino DiIorio, Playwright

Most playwrights appreciate an open conversation about their work. Transparency is crucial through all steps of development. With the help of candid discussions, writers groups, colleagues, peers, friends, audiences, and the fleeting communities of creative teams that assemble for Readings, playwrights can attain the inspiration that encourages them to continue writing.

This book is dedicated to the next generation of playwrights—and those who follow.

FOR EMERGING ARTISTS

Young writers should go out into the world and figure out who's directing and producing plays they like. Expose yourself to all the possibilities. Find different ways of working. There doesn't need to be a template. —Adam Greenfield, Associate Artistic Director, Playwrights Horizons

I learned about readings as a Yale undergraduate. They have a healthy playwriting program. We were assigned mentors, and our plays were given readings. I've also been involved as a guest artist with other colleges and universities where readings are part of the theatre department's programming. This makes a smooth transition from writing in college to entering the professional world. —Lauren Yee, Playwright

I encourage producers to let as many people in the rehearsal room as possible—dramaturgs, assistant directors, interns. It's a great learning experience. —Nan Barnett, Executive Director, National New Play Network

Actors—get out there and sing! Benefit concerts, cabarets, and other events—anywhere your work can be seen. —Cara Reichel, Producing Artistic Director, Prospect Theater Company

The writer needs a certain level of experience to understand how to hear their play. Inexperienced writers are hungry and eager and impatient with the process of new play development. The landscape is unstructured, with no clear path or trajectory. So often, experienced directors or playwright mentors can help them realize their vision, and navigate the waters. Young directors also need the opportunity to work with young writers. They need to get their hands dirty. But they need structured programs, like Ensemble Studio Theatre's Youngblood, to understand and benefit from the process. Programs like these are a great segue from the academic to the professional world. —Daniella Topol, Director

It's particularly important and helpful for young writers to hear what they've written spoken out loud. Readings can be a great opportunity for the playwrights to use their collaborators as sounding boards, and can also help early-career writers make connections to directors, actors, producers, etc. —Jojo Ruf, Managing Director, Laboratory for Global Performance and Politics, Georgetown University; former Executive Director, National New Play Network

My favorite part about National Playwriting Program readings is the feedback the playwrights get from the respondents who are invited—professional playwrights and NPP theatre educators from all over the country. Some regions work closely with the Dramatists Guild Traveling Masters Program which sends a member professional playwrights to the festival to teach workshops and dialogue with students about their experience as a professional playwright. —Nancy Lee-Painter, The Kennedy Center American College Theater Festival, National Playwriting Program Vice-Chair, Region 7

When I was at Carnegie Mellon, we did readings of new plays every week, and developed a play every semester. Milan Stitt, the chair of the theatre department, was a trailblazer. He was committed to training students about readings. There was no separation between the writer and the director. By the time we graduated, we knew how to do readings. —Jose Zayas, Director

I say to young playwrights, "Dude, you're alone. It's a lonely world out there. You have to muddle through. Don't love it too much. It doesn't love you back." You have to write for other reasons than success. You have a question in your mind that needs to be answered, or something you have to let out. And you can do that with your plays. —Gino DiIorio, Playwright

UNIONS AND GUILDS

Unions and guilds are singular of purpose: They exist to serve and to protect their members. Union rules should never be ignored. They should also never be assumed. Union regulations often pose challenges; at times, the logic of certain rules may seem arbitrary. Some union members argue that the policies harm them as much as they help them. At times, the various unions appear to work against each other, rather than collaboratively.

> *New play development, like plays themselves, is not "one size fits all." In the last six years, SDC has been working to support directors by creating guidelines and contracts for development. Readings are usually more work for directors than for actors, whose work is most often essentially limited to the rehearsal period. Our goal is to have producers understand that it's work that the director is doing.*
> Laura Penn

If a theatre, developmental lab, or producing organization uses members of any of the various unions that represent playwrights, actors, directors, singers, and musicians, the organization should follow union policies or recommendations to the letter. Even when their members are not involved, unions' and guilds' guidelines offer common-sense advice for organizations that participate in the development of new work.

Dramatists Guild of America, Actors' Equity Association, Stage Directors and Choreographers Society, American Guild of Musical Artists, American Guild of Variety Artists, SAG-AFTRA, and The American Federation of Musicians have various contracts, policies, procedures, and recommendations that pertain to their members' involvement in Readings, Workshops, and other developmental steps.

Playwrights, composers, lyricists, and librettists who are at the center of any Reading of a new play or musical are not protected by a union. The Dramatists Guild of America provides services, support, and advice, but it does not specify policies for theatres or other organizations that present developmental work by their members.

> *Non-profit theatres have a tax-free status, and accept donations to fulfill a charitable purpose. But playwrights are taxpayers.*

They are underwriting these theatres. In effect, these theatres are charging playwrights to have their work heard.

Ralph Sevush, Esq.

Union policies have changed over the years and continue to evolve. This is the case for full productions involving union members, as well as for Readings and Workshops that are more recent developments.

Today new play projects are often in development for years, with readings and workshops. SDC agreements have not kept up. The previous agreements were just not written for development. With readings and other developmental steps, we want to ensure our members receive compensation and recognition, and that their property rights are protected. We don't expect that the "right of first refusal" should always be granted in the earlier stages but a director has some skin in the game. They may spend years working on a project. The challenge is to generate agreements for development that don't restrict or encumber, but that acknowledge a director's contributions. We know that restrictions may not protect the people you're trying to protect. SDC doesn't want to hinder or complicate new play development. We just want to be sure that directors' contributions are respected.

Laura Penn

Contracts and guidelines for members may be found on the unions' websites, but the rule of thumb when using union members is for the producing organization to check the websites first, then contact the business representative of the union directly. Union rules can often be negotiated.

In addition to the promulgated Staged Reading Guidelines, some AEA contracts contain negotiated language pertaining to staged readings. Our Staged Reading Guidelines and the negotiated language in contracts have not changed. All contracts and Guidelines can be obtained by calling an AEA office and speaking to a Business Representative.

We have different arrangements with different employer/ employer groups. If anyone has questions about using Equity Actors and Stage Managers for development of a new project, we'd be happy to discuss options directly with them. If someone wants to do a developmental reading, the individual should contact AEA to discuss options based on the specifics of the project.

Maria Somma, AEA

Guild and union members are among the best in their fields. The development of new work benefits enormously from their participation. The regulations that producing organizations must follow to employ union members may be demanding, but they are outweighed by the benefits that using their members provides.

Working With Unions

It's easy to deal with the unions if you enter the negotiation with the right attitude. We're all in this together—it's not them against us. Present your case well. Always be above-board—"Here's what we want and need; Can you work with us?" It's amazing what they will do for you if you have built a relationship based on trust.

James Morgan, Producing Artistic Director,
York Theatre Company

The unions are bending over backwards, trying to find models where actors and directors working on new material can make a living while they're in development. There used to be less money in development. With musicals, what's considered a reading now is much more complicated, and the stakes are higher. If you don't continue on with the show, there are now financial protections. Producers can also look for contracts that protect the artists involved, either by being paid more, or owning a piece of the show. The jury is still out if these new contracts are working. It's all shifting and changing.

Nick Corley, Director; Actor

Unions want to work with you, to help their members work. We've negotiated with various AEA Business Reps, and have received letters of agreement without much trouble. We do right by the actors, and I think AEA knows that.

Jesse Berger, Artistic Director,
Red Bull Theater

Whether or not a playwright, director, actor, stage manager or musician should become a member of a union or a guild is a personal choice. Where theatre artists live and their level of experience are only a few of the considerations that enter into the decision. Emerging artists should research the websites carefully and contact the unions and guilds directly with any questions.

The policies of the unions and guilds directly impact many of the artists involved in new work. The health, growth, and stability of these organizations are vital to the future of new plays. Producing organizations must work effectively with them.

SELECTIONS, CUTTINGS, AND EXCERPTS

Certain organizations that present Readings (and performances) of plays and musicals stipulate that only a selection or excerpt from the piece can be performed at their festivals or showcases. National Alliance for Music Theatre, 5th Avenue Theatre's New Works at the Fifth, Village Theatre, and members of the American Association of Community Theatres are such institutions.

> At the American Association of Community Theatre's national festivals, we do cuttings from plays so that more plays can be presented. It's a time factor. Cuttings can expose more new plays to more theatres. They are an effective communicator, when done well. We also offer "how to" articles in the AACT newsletter with advice about cuttings.
>
> Julie Crawford, Executive Director,
> American Association of Community Theatre

In most cases, the organization specifies the exact length of the selection or excerpt that is allowed, along with any other stipulations and preferences, such as whether the selection can include different parts of the full piece or whether it needs to be one continuous sequence.

Certain playwrights do not permit presentations of excerpts of their work. For any published play, the producer or director should contact the publisher to obtain permission to perform a selection.

Some theatre artists challenge the purpose and effectiveness of selections and excerpts.

> At the York, we don't believe in doing "cuttings" or "selections." We only do full-length readings of musicals. Cutting a show can make a bad show look wonderful. Forty-five minutes of a show can be very misleading.
>
> James Morgan, Producing Artistic Director,
> York Theatre Company

When a cutting is required, directors, playwrights, composers, lyricists and librettists should craft the selection with care and precision. The goal is usually to interest producers, funders or theatres, and to do so, the selection needs to capture the essence of the full work.

> *When you only have a small amount of time and need to present selections, what's important is that there's still a beginning, middle and end, and that you communicate the energy of the material. Organizations or producers who request selections offer valid opportunities for new material. You need to make strong choices—clarify the story for the audience. If you have created a well thought-out presentation, a producer can tell if the story interests them and if they are intrigued by the book and score. Having passed the first hurdle, a producer will then want to read the entire thing. Hopefully they will then provide financial backing for a full reading and/or development.*
>
> Nick Corley, Director; Actor

Selections, cuttings, and excerpts, like Play Readings, can be their own distinct forms of presentation. And like Readings, while they impose challenges they also provide opportunities for production. They are a significant component of the current model of development, and theatre artists must learn how to work effectively within their margins.

A PLAYWRIGHT'S RESPONSES: A, REY PAMATMAT

1) Generally speaking, do you find readings of your work helpful in its developmental stages?

I do find readings very helpful in different stages of the writing and revising process.

2) If so, in what ways? If not, why?

Since plays are meant to exist off the page, readings are a good way to begin envisioning what I'm writing in a 3-D space with individual voices. The ease with which actors pick up action and diction also help me to understand how well I'm doing in building the characters.

3) What does it mean when people say readings let playwrights "hear their play out loud"? What does "hearing" a play mean to you?

To me, hearing the play out loud is partly about seeing if the structure, the basic machinery, works. It also partly means hearing the text, the subtext, and how they enhance each other. Often I can't really do that in my head or reading out loud to myself, because I'll always play the effect I hope a line or passage of dialogue will have rather than observing the effects it could possibly have.

4) What do you want to know from the producers going into a reading? After a reading?

As in most things, I appreciate full transparency. I prefer when producers tell me their goals for the reading: are they trying to see if parts of the play work? If an actor works in a certain role? Do they want to see what I'm like in a rehearsal room? How I work with a certain director? Is this just an opportunity for me to show off? Or is there work they feel needs to be done? And, of course, it's good to know whether the play is under consideration for programming.

Afterward, I just want to know if the goals the producers had for the reading were met or not. Occasionally, I'll ask a few specific questions to elicit feedback, but I don't generally like unsolicited feedback unless we're meeting at a separate time to have a whole discussion about the reading.

5) Do you like to be involved in the choice of director? And in casting?

For a reading I'm flexible with the director, but I prefer to choose especially for a first reading. When it's a short period of rehearsal time, it's just much easier to get things accomplished with the play if you're not also establishing a completely new partnership. The same goes with actors. I also tend to write with specific performers in mind, so readings are a good place for me to see what people can do with what I wrote for them. I don't always write all of the parts that way, but there're usually one or two roles written for friends.

6)   Do you prefer in-house/table reading, or public readings, or both?

It depends on what the goals for the reading are. I have done and learned a lot from both.

7)   At what point in a play's development is a reading most helpful to you?

I have things read pretty constantly. First versions of scenes are usually read by fellow writers in meetings of the Ma-Yi Writers Lab. When I have a rough draft, I like to hear it out loud with actors at a table, just to know what it sounds and feels like beginning to end, whether the characters work, and if there are steps in the action of the play that are missing. I often revise after that reading and then like to hear the play in front of an audience for the first time. Following the first public reading, I only usually want readings of the play if I've changed something major and need to see the effect it's having on the play, or if it's to establish a relationship with potential collaborators (director, theatre, and so on).

8)   As for the "nuts and bolts" of readings, do you prefer simple readings (sitting or standing at music stands, with little or no staging, and no props or costumes)? Or do you find "semi-staged" readings helpful?

Again, it depends on the goals. I do find semi-staged readings helpful when I've written larger plays. My last play that had a semi-staged reading was A Power Play; Or, What's-its-name at the O'Neill in 2014. That needed to be up on its feet because it involved three scenes with ten actors on stage. The only way to know whether those scenes worked was to stage it.

9)   Do you find talkbacks useful in any way? Is there a type of "talkback protocol" that you prefer? Or do you prefer other methods of feedback, such as questionnaires?

Generally, I think talkbacks are for the audience. No one in a talkback will give feedback that is useful no matter how smart they are. Which isn't to say talkbacks are completely useless. They're really great for gauging reactions and knowing what people are coming away with; you can usually listen to their feedback and figure out what you need to change. Less in terms of actually taking notes, and more in terms of re-shaping the experience when they're fixated on things you don't want them to be fixated on or they're missing things you need them to see. I'm also a big fan of talkbacks being firmly moderated by someone other than the playwright who can ask questions, stop people from talking, and limit the amount of time spent on particular topics.

10)   What advice/warnings would you give emerging playwrights about the current model of new play development, which often includes readings as a step on the path to production?

The best advice I can give is for young playwrights to understand that readings are less like auditions and more like dates. Find out what they want from the evening, be clear about what you want, and only think beyond that evening if both parties are willing to go there together. Most readings are to get to know you; they probably aren't going to do your play. So if your goal is to figure out that 10-person scene or to make sure you're shocking the audience the right way or to get the artistic director to laugh, you'll be able to learn and to do good work on your script almost every time. If the goal is get a production, then you will fail almost every time. And, just like on a date: no means no. Don't push anyone to give feedback or make promises they aren't interested in or aren't ready to give, and likewise don't solicit feedback you aren't ready to take or make promises on which you aren't interested in following up.

ADVICE FROM A CASTING DIRECTOR: TOM ROWAN

1. How can actors who have recently moved to New York or another big city get cast in Play Readings, which are usually cast through "offers"?

I would suggest finding a few theatres that do a lot of readings, go to the readings and take part in the discussions afterwards. The director, the playwright, the literary manager and artistic director of the theatre are usually all there. You can introduce yourself and get to know them. Many of these theatres have intern programs; you can apply for these, which gets you in the door. Offer to read stage directions the first couple of times, or to be a reader for auditions; that way they can get to know your work. And make friends with playwrights and directors; in casting readings, most people start by going to actors they know and trust.

2. How is acting in a Play Reading different than acting in a Full Production (apart from the obvious things like they won't be off book or in costume)? How should actors approach it differently?

There's not nearly as much rehearsal time for a reading, so you need to do some preparation on your own and come in ready to use the rehearsals as productively as possible. Make sure you understand the play going in; write down any questions you need to ask the director. Look up any words you don't know (or don't know how to pronounce) and get them down. Once I saw a reading of a play where an actor was playing an opera conductor, but he hardly knew how to pronounce any of the Italian names or musical terms in the text, which made it hard for him to be convincing as that character. Do your homework. Come in with ideas about your actions and objectives: what does your character want in the scene and what is he doing to get it? And read the play as many times as you have time for before the reading.

3. Are there certain types of actors who are more effective in Play Readings than others?

An actor in a reading needs to be very facile at reading words of the page accurately and making sense of them quickly. That's a skill that can take a long time to develop. You need to be sharp and precise with all the words and punctuation; read exactly what is there, rather than just glancing down and getting the sense of the line and then half-adlibbing it. A playwright needs to hear what he or she really wrote. You have to be bold, and able to make active choices very quickly, and also be flexible enough to turn on a dime if the director or playwright asks for something different. You need to be able to read fast; because there are no visuals, a reading has to be paced quicker than a full performance. Immediate cue pickup and energized, quick but clear speech are very important. And you should be genuinely interested in writers and developing new work; you are putting yourself in the service of the script, rather than using it as an opportunity to show off your own skills.

4.　Do you think it's appropriate for actors to follow up with Producers, Playwrights, and/or Directors after a play reading?

Sure; a quick Thank You card or e-mail is great.

6.　Do you have any advice for Stage Directions Readers?

Remember to pick up your cues quickly and read with energy. You are the storyteller so you have to enjoy the words and the excitement of leading the audience into the world of the play. If you read in a flat, uninflected voice you will sap all the energy out of the scene. As the reader, you are largely responsible for the pace of the whole evening, and you need to drive it and keep the story moving forward.

INTERNATIONAL READINGS: HORACIO PÉREZ

Introduction

My name is Horacio Pérez. I am a theatre artist from Chile. I'm 32 years old. I studied acting at the Theatre Department of the Universidad de Chile, and in 2011 I received a scholarship from the government of my country to study a Master of Arts in Arts Politics at New York University. After I finished my graduate studies I did an internship at the Public Theater in NYC, where I worked as an intern in the Literary Department, and where I saw countless readings of plays, a genre that I wasn't too familiar with, because they are not such a developed language in Chilean theatre as they are in American theatre. Currently I work in the Theatre Department of the Universidad de Chile (where I studied) as a professor and a coordinator for the Acting major.

My interest in readings started while working at the Public, hearing all these readings in a language that wasn't my own. Beyond the quality of the plays I saw, what fascinated me was the event of watching a group of actors reading a play, because I considered it a very "democratic" practice—an idea I will develop further very soon—and because it offered a very concrete way of dealing with the whole reality/fiction/representation crisis I had in my head as a theatre director, related to the fact that I don't really believe in the convention of the fourth wall (and I feel more related to performance or other ways of post-dramatic theatre). In a reading, no one is lying to the spectator, because no one is pretending that the stage is a living room or that the characters "don't know" they are being observed. For me, readings were most honest, and they can give a sense of authorship to the spectator. In the reading all the images are constructed inside the spectator's mind, and that seems much more interesting for me, because each spectator constructs their own version of what they hear. The first time I directed a reading was in 2011, and the play (entitled "Hungarians" by Spanish playwright Alberto Conejero) posited the image of a "burning greenhouse." And for me, the most interesting part was the fact that spectators created their own burning greenhouses in their heads, and that image only existed there. That fact even relates (to me, and this is also a very personal approach) to that premise from the Greek tragedy where the violent scenes occur outside the stage and are just described by some character, so the audience can construct their own violent scene in their heads, a scene that can be much more powerful and horrific than a faked staged action because it's drawn by imagination.

In 2014 I developed a project with my friend Isidora Stevenson (actress, playwright, and director), in which we curate a cycle of readings of Chilean plays from different authors and periods around a topic in common, as a way of researching how authors from different times and styles reflected around a same topic. The readings were shown in non-conventional spaces (such as a hair salon or a hotel room) and directed by young directors from our same generations. The title of the project is "Correr la Voz," which means "to spread the word," but literally means "to move the voice" (a game of words that, unfortunately, has no translation to the English language). In 2014 we created the first episode, and on 2015 we will do the second.

For the first episode of my project "Correr la Voz," Isidora and me chose five Chilean plays that reflected around the practice of theatre, and we invited five directors to create a 20 minute reading in a non-theatre space we assigned them: a restaurant, a hair salon, a hotel room, an art gallery and an old house. There were no costumes or light design, and the director must assume the spatial conditions of the given location, without altering them. In that sense, the voice of the actors is the main scenic resource, creating a tension between the material presence of the architecture of each space and ephemeral presence of the voice. Because the voice is the main tool and that tool is "moved" from its original space (the theatre) we intend to take the theatre outside the theatre, without the mise en scene as a mediator between play and audience. And the reading seems like the perfect format, because it doesn't need a long schedule of rehearsal or any kind of costume, scenography or lighting device. All we need is the written words, the voices of the actors and the spaces to contain the readings. In that sense the reading becomes "democratic," because they can be accessible for everyone (because the readings were, of course, presented for free). In that sense, we "spread the words" with the audience; the word of a dramatic material that is part of Chilean history and culture, the word of authors that came before us and wrote about Chilean identity through the lens of theatre. In that sense, those words become accessible to audience.

The idea of the project is to develop the creative possibilities of a reading, so it can be not just a way of sharing written material with an audience, but also a possibility of creative and artistic research for both the directors and us, the curators of the project.

Questions

1) Generally speaking, do you find readings helpful in its developmental stages of a new play? If so, in what ways? If not, why?

In general, I think that a Reading is a very helpful way of developing new plays, because the audience can give feedback regarding things that the playwrights "cannot see" anymore, because they are too attached to the play and it's hard for them to have a distance from the material they are writing. In Chile, the practice of readings is not as developed as it is in the United States or Europe, and many times you go to the theatre and you see a new play and you talk to the author about impressions, and you realize that the play was never shown to anyone before, so some elements are redundant, unnecessary or not as mature as they could be. In that sense, I think the audience of a reading can play the role of a curator or editor, an outside observer.

2) What does it mean when people say readings let playwrights "hear their play out loud"? What does "hearing" a play mean to you?

My theatre professor Fernando González Mardones (a prominent figure in Chilean theatre, who is an Professor Emeritus from the Universidad de Chile and received the National Prize of Arts in 2005—the highest recognition an artist can receive in Chile, given by the President) usually tells his students that there is no way to write a tense silence or an onomatopoeia. As an example he inhales and exhales in a very tense-emotional way, and then asks "How can a writer write that?" Written words are very different from words said out loud, because they are different materialities. When a written text is read out loud new meanings appear, and what someone wrote with one intention can easily be interpreted in another way by someone else. By reading plays out loud, writers can realize that something they thought had one interpretation can have another, or they can even discover new meanings to the same words they wrote. Hearing a play means that the words are alive, that they have a certain materiality, a shape, an emotion . . . things that cannot be contained in the paper because grammatical signs cannot contain them. A written play is a play in the sense that it has scenic virtuality, that can exist in present time. A play is complete when it's said by a live body, because it becomes present and alive.

3) Do you want the playwright to be involved in the choice of director? And in casting?

In Chilean theatre is very rare for a playwright not to choose the director of his/her own play, because the professional circuit is very small, so it's hard to be in that situation where a total stranger wants to direct your play or that some producer decides to produce a play because he likes it and calls a director. It happens, but not very often. In that sense, my opinion is that is useful because I haven't really been in that other situation. As for the cast, I think that sometimes is useful for the author to be involved, but not always, because (as I said before) is interesting when directors have different interpretations of some given material.

For my project "Correr la Voz," for example, we decide "who directs what" because usually the plays have already been staged, and the purpose is to "revisit" them, regardless of whether the playwright is alive or not.

4) Do you (and your audiences) prefer in-house/table reading, or public readings, or both?

I'm not really familiar with the house/table concept. If it is what I think, I imagine they can be helpful for those in charge, but I totally prefer public readings, because they provide a wider range of spectators.

5) At what point in a play's development is a reading most helpful to you?

Whenever the authors feel they have reached some point of development or completion, and they feel it could be useful to have some feedback. A professor who was a painter told me that "sometimes you need to take to steps away from your painting in order to see it clearly and see what is missing," and in this case, I think that inviting an audience to hear would be a useful way of stepping away from the play and see it more clearly.

6) As for the "nuts and bolts" of readings, do you prefer simple readings (sitting or standing at music stands, with little or no staging, and no props or costumes)? Or do you find "semi-staged" readings helpful?

I have struggled a lot with that question. As readings are not fully developed in Chile as a language, directors always try to "spice up" the readings, moving the actors, using costumes or light effects, making actions. And that's because they think that the audience will "get bored" or "won't understand important facts of the play" (like space changes or significant actions), and this would be a way of making them more interesting. But for me, those are excuses, because they hide the original play, as if they don't trust the material enough or don't consider it interesting. But in my personal opinion (and taste), the less produced the reading, the more significant and radical it is, because the text becomes more important. When directors start being "creative," the interest diverges from the text, and therefore, the text is no longer the main point of attention.

In the project "Correr la Voz," fortunately, the directors have accepted the rules of the game and they have accepted simple readings as an esthetic choice . . . but that's mainly because I have been very clear in my intention they do it that way.

7) Do you find talkbacks useful in any way? Is there a type of "talkback protocol" that you prefer? Do you prefer other methods of feedback, such as questionnaires?

I think they are useful as long as everyone understands that is not like a "let's all create this play together" kind of experience. What I mean is that everyone—we see a play or a movie or any work of art, it's hard to avoid the "I would've done it this way" kind of comment (mainly because the piece we are observing was done by another person and not by ourselves). A talkback can be useful if the playwright takes just what he or she wants to, because everyone will give ideas, observations, suggestions or ask different things, because we are different people. It is important that the playwright is not obsessed with pleasing everyone in the audience, because (thankfully) that is impossible.

8) What advice/warnings would you give emerging playwrights about the current model of new play development, which often includes readings as a step on the path to production?

Not to be afraid of showing a play that is unfinished or in process, because a play is never really finished, nor even after its premiere, and if you show it to other people they can help you to find what your play is about, where is it going, not just in terms of plot or character development, but in deeper, more conceptual ways. Playwrights are usually very careful of not showing a play until it's "done," but sometimes you need others to tell you what is missing, what is not necessary, what people understand. A play is never done because it's always in movement, because it's alive and it only exists in the present.

In that sense, I think playwright should "care less" about their plays. In Chile, because the readings model is not as fully developed as it is in other countries, playwrights find it very hard to read an unfinished play, because of what "people may think." They don't see it as an opportunity. My advice would be to understand that a play is a provocation to the director, the actors, the designer and everyone involved in a production of a play: a provocation for other scenes to appear onstage. So a staged reading would be a way of testing what a certain play constructs in spectator's minds and bodies.

9) Is there anything you'd like to say about the challenges and rewards of presenting readings in a place where they are not normally done?

Readings as a format are not fully developed in Chile. They have always existed, of course, but their existence is usually related to Playwriting Festivals or contests, but they are not as common as they are in the United States. And I think that they should be, because they can be a great opportunity not only to get feedback about a certain piece, but also to get money, producers, promotion, etc., as I learned while working in the Public Theater. As a spectator, I was unfamiliar with them as well, and at the beginning of my internship it was fascinating to see how developed they are in NY, and how they are used for both artistic and production purposes. American theatre has a very complex model of production, and readings play an integral role in it; a role I'm trying to develop more in my country. Fortunately, many young Chileans are studying abroad like I did (because the Chilean government has a great Scholarship system that allows many people to attend graduate school in foreign countries), so new models of production and creation are being installed in Chilean culture, and readings are an example. In that way, I am aware that I'm not the only Chilean artist exploring readings as a valid format, and that makes me happy.

In that sense, the main challenge is the one I described earlier: that people are not really familiar with the language, so they don't trust that a reading will be interesting enough and they feel the urge to make it "more interesting." I am rehearsing a reading right now as an actor, and in the first meeting the director told us that he was planning to have between 8 and 10 rehearsals, and all the other actors were worried because they thought it wasn't enough. As they are not familiar with the format they feel a little intimidated by it, because they want to make "more" or they want the reading to look like a staged play. It's hard to convince directors and actors (and playwrights!) that a reading is just that: a reading. A reading is way of approaching a text. It's a circumstance, not a problem. Is like when you do a play with no money; instead of pretending you have money, you should accept that you don't have money for production, and the production should use that as part of the concept.

The same challenge applies to the audiences. Audiences are not familiar with the format either, so they don't get why they should attend a play in which actors don't move and they don't even know their texts so they have to read them. They find it boring, because they are used to the spectacle.

The reward is, of course, the same one: creators and spectators are not familiar with readings, and that is a huge possibility of exploration. It's rewarding to see that actors and directors and playwrights are opening themselves to this possibility and they are more willing to show "unfinished" work, or works sustained just in a group of actors seated in line with papers in their hands.

In Chile theatre is not a business, and for many theatre creators it's impossible to make a living from theatre. So it's rewarding to see a format that allows theatre to get produced (as I've seen with my own eyes in the theatre circuit of another country) is getting more attention and could become a way of producing plays in the future.

PLAYS USED IN THE TEXT: SYNOPSES AND SCENES

"Death By Design" by Rob Urbinati

The Play: Playwright Edward Bennett and his actress wife Sorel retreat to their country home following a disastrous opening night. Various guests arrive unexpectedly, and when one of them is murdered, it's left to Brigit, the wily Irish maid, to figure out "whodunnit."

The Scene: Victoria Van Roth, a bohemian and Sorel's dear friend, improvises a modern dance, partly to humiliate Walter Pearce, a politician who has come to woo Sorel. Edward, Sorel and Eric, the socialist, are given actions to perform, as Brigit, the maid, and Jack, the chauffeur watch, perplexed.

"Under The Mango Tree" by Carmen Rivera

The Play: Lena, a twelve-year old tomboy from New York, is sent to Puerto Rico to spend the summer with her feisty, widowed grandmother, Fela. Gradually, as Lena matures into a young woman, she and Fela learn to transform their anger and find the love they thought was missing from their lives.

The Scenes:

Scene 3: Lena and Fela get to know one another.

Scene 18: The day of the Fiesta. Gloria, Lena's older cousin, has made a dress for her. Belen is Fela's closet friend, and her grandson Junior has befriended Lena. Felix, an older man who bought the property next door, has a romantic interest in Fela. Gradually, Junior's interest in Lena also turns romantic.

"Mama's Boy" by Rob Urbinati

The Play: Lee Harvey Oswald returns to Texas after having defected to Russia. His mother Marguerite uses all her powers to get him back into her clutches. Lee retreats into a secret world, which concerns his mother, his brother, and his Russian wife Marina. Lee is arrested for assassinating President Kennedy, intensifying the internal family struggles.

The Scene: Lee is demoralized by his attempts to make a new life in America. Despite his love for his wife and infant child, he explodes with rage at Marina, who has let Marguerite into their home against his wishes.

"Salt in A Wound" by Melissa Maxwell

The Play: A widow struggling to raise six children on her own rules her house with an iron fist. Julia is a talented dancer with big dreams. However, being the oldest daughter, Ma has other plans for Julia's future. Julia, shackled by family responsibility and social mores, struggles to find freedom and personal happiness.

The Scene: Jitter tries to convince Julia that he loves her and is the man for her. Julia is tentative and, as always, she's afraid of how her mother would react.

"Samsara" by Lauren Yee

The Play: Katie and Craig are having a baby with a surrogate who lives in India. A month before the baby's due date, Craig reluctantly travels to the subcontinent, where he meets Suraiya, their less-than-thrilled surrogate. As all three "parents" anxiously wait for the baby to be born, flights of fancy attack them from all sides.

The Scene: During an ultrasound, Craig and the Doctor examine the fetus on the monitor. Only Suraiya sees the "amorphous blob" as a fully-grown Indian man, Amit, who tries to befriend her.

"The Flood" Music and Lyrics by Peter Mills, Book by Cara Reichel

The Play: The inhabitants of a small town struggle against the rising tide of the Mississippi River that could wipe them off the map. "The Flood" examines cycles of devastation and rebirth, as the community faces adversity and attempts to rebound from disaster.

The Scene: As floodwaters slowly cover the town, Curtis tries to persuade Ezekiel Wright to evacuate. Wright's daughter Alice tells her father that her younger, mildly autistic sister Rosemary has disappeared. As they search frantically for her, nearby, Rosemary trips and falls, and is consumed by the River.

INDEX

Page numbers in *italic* indicate diagrams and photographs.

entrances, initial positions, intermission, bows and exits 150–151
Equity *see* Actors Equity Association
Esbjornsen, David: actors 154; audiences 179; music stands 47; plays served by readings 4; programming 7–8; reading usefulness 16; talkbacks 181
Eugene O'Neill Theatre Center 2, 3
extended stage directions 110–120, *114, 116–117, 119*

Fields, Dan: process versus product 160; reading usefulness 17
Finn, Haley: developmental labs 161; directors 26
follow-up: actors 190; directors 189–190; emails, eblasts and social media 190–191; playwrights 186–190; producers 186–191
foreign language 136–137
Frankel, Elizabeth: follow-up 187; limitations of readings 19; programming 7; talkbacks 5
Funkenbusch, Phil: nondevelopmental readings 174

Garza, Lisa: reading usefulness 16
gestures and physicalization: consistency 100; extended stage directions in "Death By Design:" 110–120, *114, 116, 117, 119*; intimacy in "Salt In A Wound:" 120–128, *121, 123, 125–126*; motivation 54, 96, 147; musicals and operas 170–171; standing versus sitting 54; suspending 97; unconventional stage directions and unusual behavior in "Samsara:" 138–147, *141, 143, 145–146*; in "Under the Mango Tree:" 96–109, *98–99, 101, 103, 105, 107–108*; violence in "Mama's Boy:" 128–137, *130, 132, 134; see also* editing stage directions
goals with readings 6, 10, 15, 23, 36, 40, 94, 162, 163, 184, 199, 205–207
Great American Musicals in Concert 173
Greenfield, Adam: blocking 44–45; emerging artists 197; goals with readings 6; limitations of readings 19; play development 193; programming 8; stage directions 78
guidelines 28–29, 42, 43, 84, 199–201
Gupton, Janet: auditions 38; enhancement 42; playwright and director discussions 32–33

industry reading 11
in-house reading 7, 9–10; 15, 165

international readings 29, 41, 161, 188, 211–215
intimacy 120–128, *121, 123, 125–126*
inviting industry 6, 162–163

Joseph, Rajiv: directors 26; notes 185; reading usefulness 1–2; talkbacks 184
Judson Poets' Theatre, 2

Kazan, Elia 2
KCACT Festival, KCACTF *see* Kennedy Center American College Theater Festival
Kennedy Center American College Theater Festival (KCACTF) 1, 9, 26–27, 29, 32–33, 38, 42, 185

LaMama Experimental Theatre Club, 2
Lark Play Development Center 2, 182
Lee-Painter, Nancy: auditions 38; directors 26–27; emerging artists 198; guidelines 29; nondevelopmental readings 174
LGBTQ writers 18–19, 27
libretto readings 165, 167
lighting 148–149
literary staff 3, 5, 8, 9–10, 18, 20, 21, 37, 181, 187, 188, 193, 197
Living Theatre 2

Marsh, Amy Rose: audiences 179, playwrights 194–195; stage directions 79
memorization 151–152, 173
minority writers 27
moderators 25, 182–183, 206
Mollenkamp, Julie: guidelines 29; talkbacks 185
monologues in readings 156–157
Morgan, Ian: audiences 94; casting 35; editing stage directions 80; limitations of readings 20; play development 20; programming 7; readings as performance 196; simplicity 40
Morgan, James: Actors Equity Association 201; auditions 34; directors 27; inviting industry 162–163; reading usefulness 18; selections 203
multi-character scenes 67–74 *see also* placement and movement of actors
musicals and operas: additional rehearsal time 160–166; casting 167; development 164–166; internal stage directions 170–171; libretto readings 165; materials 167, *168–169*; nondevelopmental readings 173–174; overview 164–165; piano/vocal workshops 165–166; process versus product 160–161; recorded score 165; selections 164, 203–204; staging

222 *Index*

requirements and restrictions 164; workshops 1, 11, 17, 34, 160, 164, 166

music cues 148–150

music stands: actor adjustments 43, *51, 91–92,* 156; additional stands 63, 67, *68, 69, 70, 71, 72, 73,* 74, *75–76;* angling *49–54, 52, 53, 55, 58,* 67, *68,* 72, 97, *99, 129, 130, 132, 134,* 156; clip-on lights 149; height 49, *50, 51, 55, 58;* number and placement 47, 49; overview 11, 17–18, 28, 40–45, *46;* sharing 120, *123, 125–126;* stage directions reader 60–63, *61–62;* views on 47; *see also* placement and movement of actors

National Alliance for Musical Theatre 1

National New Play Network (NNPN) 1, 9, 18, 28, 80, 194, 197

Negro Ensemble Company (NEC) 3

Newbury, Kevin: opera workshops 166; process versus product 161

New Group 7

New York Theatre Workshop 183

Nguyen, Don; goals with readings 5; limitations of readings 20; reading usefulness 16; talkbacks 184; writers groups 195

NNPN *see* National New Play Network

nondevelopmental readings: cast size 172–173; considerations 175; musicals 173–174; other venues 174; overview 10–11; plays 172–173; rewrites 174

nonprofit theaters 2–3, 9, 164, 189, 193, 195

notes 2–3, 5, 31, 93, 153, 155, 158, 185, 186, 187, 188, 190, 195, 206 *see also* rewrites; talkbacks

novelistic and poetic stage directions 78, 138–139, 142, 147

O'Connor, Susan Louise: asking questions 155; moderators and talkbacks 183; music stands 47; reading usefulness 17–18, 154

Odets, Clifford 2

Off-Broadway 2, 193–195

offers for play readings 23–24, 35–38, 209

Off-Off-Broadway 2, 193, 195

O'Neill, Eugene 2

O'Neill *see* Eugene O'Neill Theatre Center

Open Theater 2

Opera Fusion: New Works 164

operas *see* musicals and operas

opera workshops 166–167

pacing and pauses 15, 40, 41, 78, 133, 152, 156, 157, 158, 210

Pamatmat, A. Rey 205–207

passage of time in stage directions 133, 135, 183

pencils and highlighters 63, 69, 92, 122 148, 155, 156, 157

Penn, Laura: agreements and contracts 199, 200; directors 189; moderators and talkbacks 182; reading usefulness 17, 200

Pérez, Horacio 211–215

physicalization *see* gestures and physicalization

piano/vocal workshops 165–166

Pinter, Harold 78

pitch *see* process versus product

placement and movement of actors 28–29, 40–45, 63–76, *64–66, 68, 71, 73, 75–76; see also* gestures and physicalization; music stands

play readings: accepting offer for 23–24; as auditions 6–8, 160, 175; chairs 57–60, *58–59,* 63; clothing, hair, and makeup 28, 74–77; dissenting voices 3–8; enhancement 42–43; essential nature of 1–2; goals with 6, 10, 15, 23, 36, 40, 94, 162, 163, 184, 199, 205–207; history of 2–3; international readings 211–215; investors and producers at 6, 162–163; listening to 21; nondevelopmental 172–175; overview 11, 43–45; as performance 8, 196; placement and movement of actors 44–45, 63–67, *64–66, 68, 70, 73, 75–76;* plays served by 4; programming 6–8, 18–19, 161, 179; proposed model 43–44; props 29, 41, 43, 47, 82, 83, 85, 92, 96–109, 115, *116, 117,* 118, *119,* 120, 133, 152; reading draft with struck-through edits 83–84, 86, *95,* 167; simplicity 40–42, 43, 74; stage directions reader; 60, 84, 85, *107, 108, 114, 121, 126, 132, 141, 142, 143, 146,* 157–159; standing versus sitting 54–57; stools 54–56, *55–56;* types of 9–11; usefulness 1–2, 15–16; venue and 45; *see also* actors; development; directors; gestures and physicalization; music stands; playwrights; producers; retreat positions

playwrights: additional rehearsal time 162; attachments 23, 24 189, 190, 200; audiences and talkbacks 183–185; casting 38–39; cast size 172–173; determining scene significance 112; discussion with producers 24–25; discussions with directors 32–33, 35; earning money 194–195; follow-up discussions 186–188; going public 15–16; incorporating voice into readings 147; minority and LGBTQ writers 27; notes 2–3, 5, 31, 93, 153,